# Cambridge Elements ☰

Elements in Cognitive Linguistics
edited by
Sarah Duffy
*Northumbria University*
Nick Riches
*Newcastle University*

# LANGUAGE CHANGE AND COGNITIVE LINGUISTICS

## *Case Studies from the History of Russian*

Tore Nesset
*UiT The Arctic University of Norway*

CAMBRIDGE
UNIVERSITY PRESS

Shaftesbury Road, Cambridge CB2 8EA, United Kingdom

One Liberty Plaza, 20th Floor, New York, NY 10006, USA

477 Williamstown Road, Port Melbourne, VIC 3207, Australia

314–321, 3rd Floor, Plot 3, Splendor Forum, Jasola District Centre,
New Delhi – 110025, India

103 Penang Road, #05–06/07, Visioncrest Commercial, Singapore 238467

Cambridge University Press is part of Cambridge University Press & Assessment,
a department of the University of Cambridge.

We share the University's mission to contribute to society through the pursuit of
education, learning and research at the highest international levels of excellence.

www.cambridge.org
Information on this title: www.cambridge.org/9781009013536

DOI: 10.1017/9781009031554

First published 2022

*A catalogue record for this publication is available from the British Library.*

ISBN 978-1-009-01353-6 Paperback
ISSN 2633-3325 (online)
ISSN 2633-3317 (print)

Additional resources for this publication at www.cambridge.org/nesset-resources

# Language Change and Cognitive Linguistics

## Case Studies from the History of Russian

Elements in Cognitive Linguistics

DOI: 10.1017/9781009031554
First published online: November 2022

Tore Nesset
*UiT The Arctic University of Norway*
**Author for correspondence:** Tore Nesset, tore.nesset@uit.no

**Abstract:** The purpose of this Element is to bring together three subfields of the language sciences: cognitive, historical (diachronic), and Russian linguistics. Although diachrony has inspired a number of important works in recent years, historical linguistics is still under-represented in cognitive linguistics, and the most influential publications mainly concern the history of English. This is an unfortunate bias, especially since its lack of morphological complexity makes English a typologically unusual language. In this Element, the author demonstrates that Russian has a lot to offer the historically oriented cognitive linguist, given its well-documented history and complex phonology and morphosyntax. Through seven case studies, the author illustrates the relevance of four basic tenets of Cognitive Grammar: the cognitive, semiotic, network, and usage-based commitments.

This Element also has a video abstract: www.cambridge.org/nesset

**Keywords:** cognitive linguistics, Cognitive Grammar, historical linguistics, Russian, corpus data

ISBNs: 9781009013536 (PB), 9781009031554 (OC)
ISSNs: 2633-3325 (online), 2633-3317 (print)

# Contents

# 1 Introduction

Most speakers of a language notice that their language is changing, and they find it annoying. Young people feel that their grandparents speak in an old-fashioned way. People of my generation notice that our children and grandchildren speak differently, often in a partly incomprehensible way. All living languages acquire new words, while old words gradually go out of use. Take *sportswashing*. Just a few years ago, this word was not in common use, although the practice of using important sport events to improve the reputation of a totalitarian regime has been around for generations. However, the changes do not only concern words. Pronunciation also changes with time, and so do grammatical patterns. Therefore, for a theory of language, few questions are more important than understanding why and how language changes.

Since cognitive linguistics has opened up a number of new perspectives on language and linguistics, it seems likely that a cognitive approach may shed new light on language change. For this reason, it is unfortunate that historical linguistics is under-represented in cognitive linguistics. Although cognitive linguistics has witnessed a number of important publications about diachrony in recent years (e.g., Bybee 2007a; Traugott and Trousdale 2013; Hilpert 2013; Diessel 2019; Sommerer and Smirnova 2020), it is still fair to say that language change has received less attention than it deserves. The aim of this Element is to show that cognitive linguistics has valuable implications for language change. I will take four theoretical commitments as my starting point and discuss their relevance for diachronic linguistics through seven case studies from the history of Russian. In this introduction, I first present the cognitive, semiotic, network, and usage-based commitments (Section 1.1), and then motivate the choice of Russian as the language under scrutiny (Section 1.2). Section 1.3 offers a brief presentation of the seven case studies that will make it easier to navigate the following sections.

## 1.1 Four Commitments

In order to explore the relevance of cognitive linguistics for language change, I structure my discussion around the following four commitments that represent cornerstones in cognitive linguistics:

(1)     The cognitive commitment:
        Language is shaped by domain-general cognitive processes.

(2)     The semiotic commitment:
        Language is analysed in terms of bipolar representations that connect form and meaning (and nothing else).

(3)        The network commitment:
           The bipolar linguistic representations of a language constitute one large
           network – the 'constructicon'.

(4)        The usage-based commitment:
           Knowledge of language emerges from language use.

A section is devoted to each theoretical commitment. In each section, I will present and discuss the relevant commitment and then explore its implications for historical linguistics in one or two detailed case studies.

The commitments in (1) through (4) are likely to be shared by the whole cognitive linguistics community, and my goal is to create a narrative that will be relevant for all scholars interested in cognitive linguistics, broadly defined. For the sake of coherence and focus, I will use Langacker's (1987, 1991a, 2008, 2013) Cognitive Grammar as my point of departure. My case studies mostly concern *grammatical* change, and Langacker's model is therefore a perfect fit, since it is arguably the most holistic model of grammar in cognitive linguistics. However, although I will draw on Langacker's insights and terminology, I will not use more theoretical apparatus than is required to convey my message, and all terms will be carefully explained and related to the nomenclature of other varieties of cognitive linguistics. This is a text about ideas, not about details of linguistic representations.

While the four commitments in (1) to (4) capture important aspects of cognitive linguistics, other theoretical issues could have been included. Die-hard enthusiasts of cognitive semantics might, for instance, miss metaphor, which is central to cognitive linguistics and relevant for language change (Bybee 2015: 135–6). However, metaphor has not been at centre stage in Langacker's research, nor has metaphor been the focus of my own diachronic studies of Russian. Metaphor will therefore not figure prominently in the following.

Language change does not happen in a vacuum and studying historical linguistics without drawing on insights from sociolinguistics is futile. Unfortunately, much like historical linguistics, sociolinguistics is an under-represented field in cognitive linguistics. For this reason, sociolinguistics will not figure prominently in the following sections. For discussion of the relationship between cognitive linguistics and sociolinguistics, see Geeraerts (2016), Nesset (2016a), and Schmid (2016, 2020).

## 1.2 Why Russian?

As mentioned, diachrony is under-represented in cognitive linguistics, although language change has received increasing attention in recent years. However, most studies of language change in cognitive linguistics address topics in the history of English. As pointed out by Schmid (2020: 11), this bias is unfortunate, because its lack of morphological complexity makes English a typologically specific language. For this reason, I have chosen to illustrate the four commitments on the basis of case studies from Russian.

Russian features a complex case system, and its gender system has received considerable attention in theoretical linguistics (Corbett 1991, 2006). When it comes to verbs, the Russian aspectual system is notorious for its complexity (Dickey 2000; Zaliznjak and Šmelev 2000; Janda et al. 2013). Both in the nominal and verbal systems there are numerous interesting examples of language change that merit the attention of general linguists but are nevertheless little known outside the field of Russian and Slavic linguistics. The seven case studies we will explore in the following sections involve both the nominal and verbal systems (morphology and syntax) – and, in addition, one case study concerns phonological change. Taken together, the case studies provide a good illustration of the implications of Cognitive Grammar for language change.

One reason that makes Russian particularly suitable for the study of language change is the fact that Russian has a well-documented history, and that we have access to digital resources that facilitate qualitative and quantitative analysis of language change in Russian. Of particular importance for the present study is the Russian National Corpus, a large family of electronic corpora with advanced search functions. The main corpus, which forms the basis for most of the case studies to be pursued in the following, contains approximately 340 million words (as of September 2021) and provides a good basis for the study of language change over the last two centuries.[1] Six out of seven case studies involve data from the Russian National Corpus.

## 1.3 Seven Case Studies

Cognitive linguistics is all about using authentic data. Instead of resorting to abstract theorizing based on cherry-picked examples, I will invite you on an extensive journey through the history of Russian. I will illustrate the four commitments by means of seven detailed case studies listed in Table 1. In order to make it easier to navigate the following sections, I provide brief presentations of each case study here.

The so-called jer shift is the only sound change we will explore. We follow the development of the two lax vowels /ĭ, ŭ/ ('jers'), which either disappeared or merged with /e, o/ in Old East Slavic.[2] Is it possible to say something new about

---

[1] The Russian National Corpus is available at www.ruscorpora.ru.

[2] I use the term 'Old East Slavic' instead of the traditional term 'Old Russian', since the latter is a misnomer, insofar as we are dealing with the ancestor of not only modern Russian, but also Belarusian and Ukrainian.

**Table 1** Overview of case studies

| Case study | Commitment | Section |
| --- | --- | --- |
| Jer shift: lax vowels and rhythmic organization of language | Cognitive | 2.2 |
| Decade construction rivalry: accusative vs locative | Cognitive | 2.3 |
| Analogy in verbs: suffixes *-a, -aj* and *-nu* | Semiotic | 3.2 |
| Feminine numeral construction: *-yx* vs *-ye* | Semiotic | 3.3 |
| Semelfactive verbs: expanding network for verbs in *-nu* | Network | 4.2 |
| Case marking of objects: multiple motivation of accusative vs genitive | Usage-based | 5.2 |
| S-curves and numerals: more on the *-yx* vs *-ye* rivalry | Usage-based | 5.3 |

a sound change that has been thoroughly described by generations of Slavic linguists? Yes. Since the jer shift involves the rhythmic organization of language in trochaic feet, the shift illustrates how language is shaped by a domain-general property (rhythm), as stated in the cognitive commitment. Cognitive Grammar clearly shows the limitations of the traditional approach to the jer shift.

Russian has two ways to express that something took place within a decade (e.g., 'in the twenties'). One construction uses the accusative case, the other the locative (prepositional) case. Situations where a language has two ways of conveying the same content tend to be unstable over time, and three diachronic scenarios are likely. First, one construction may oust its rival (levelling). Second, both rivals may survive, but in different varieties of the language (sociolinguistic differentiation). Third, the two rivals may develop different meanings over time (semantic differentiation). However, in actual reality, the three scenarios are not alternatives. Very often actual change is a combination of the three scenarios. The Russian decade constructions show how a cognitive linguist can study such combined scenarios. Importantly, the case study relates to the cognitive commitment, demonstrating that Cognitive Grammar's strong focus on individual cognition does not prevent us from considering the role of social factors in language change.

Section 3 explores two case studies that are relevant for the semiotic commitment of Cognitive Grammar. With its strong emphasis on meaning, Cognitive Grammar makes us expect analogical change among linguistic items with the same meaning, while analogy is predicted to be blocked for linguistic items with different meanings. Russian verbs illustrate this. Analogical change is shown to take place in the case of the two synonymous verb suffixes *-a* and *-aj*, where a number of verbs with the *-a* suffix are in the process of adopting the productive *-aj* suffix. By contrast, analogy does not take place for verbs with the two homonymous suffixes *-nu*.

Also relevant for the semiotic commitment is the development of a feminine numeral construction in Russian. The morphosyntax of Russian numerals is notorious for its complexity, but it is possible to make sense of a series of seemingly unrelated changes if we keep in mind that the main purpose of language is to convey meaning. The common denominator for the changes in question is the development of a separate feminine construction that expresses that the quantified noun is feminine.

In Section 4, which addresses the network commitment, we return to one of the *-nu* suffixes discussed in Section 3.2. Verbs where *-nu* expresses a single punctual event such as to cough once belong to the so-called semelfactive aktionsart. Over time the suffix has spread to a number of new types of verbs. Since this development can be insightfully described as an expanding category network, the history of the semelfactive aktionsart illustrates the value of the network commitment in historical linguistics.

The two case studies in Section 5 address the usage-based commitment of Cognitive Grammar. Russian has a group of verbs that combine with objects in the accusative or genitive. This variation is conditioned by a number of different factors that can be studied on the basis of corpus data, illustrating how language is shaped by language use in a bottom-up fashion.

The final case study demonstrates the importance of quantitative analysis of corpus data in historical linguistics. Returning to numeral constructions, we explore the competition between the adjectival suffixes *-yx* and *-ye* in quantified phrases of the type 'two new apartments'. The former suffix has become the rule for masculine and neuter nouns, whereas the latter is now dominant for nouns of feminine gender. Both developments arguably follow an S-shaped curve, with a slow start, then a steep rise before the curve flattens out towards the end of the period.

## 2 The Cognitive Commitment

### 2.1 What Is the Cognitive Commitment?

Possibly the most important tenet of Cognitive Grammar (and cognitive linguistics in general) is the cognitive commitment, that is, the idea that language is shaped by domain-general cognitive processes. Langacker writes:

> Compared with formal approaches, cognitive linguistics stands out by resisting the imposition of boundaries between language and other psychological phenomena. Insofar as possible, linguistic structure is seen as drawing on other, more basic systems and abilities (e.g. perception, memory,

categorization) from which it cannot be segregated. Rather than constituting a distinct, self-contained entity (a separate 'module' or 'mental faculty'), language is viewed as an integral facet of cognition. (Langacker 2008: 8)

This is a radical position, since, as pointed out by Langacker, the cognitive commitment sets Cognitive Grammar (and, more broadly, cognitive and functional linguistics) apart from the Chomskyan tradition that has emphasized the separation of language from other cognitive abilities (Fodor 1983; Chomsky 1986). Since Langacker formulated his position, considerable progress has been made in cognitive science, but Cognitive Grammar's cognitive commitment is still a viable position. Fedorenko and Shain (2021: 526), who review a body of recent work on language comprehension, state:

'For example, in any sentence containing a non-local dependency between words, the first dependent has to be retrieved from memory when the second dependent is encountered. These kinds of operations are also invoked in other domains of perception and cognition, including object recognition, numerical and spatial reasoning, music perception, social cognition, and task planning'.

However, Fedorenko and Shain point out that it does not follow from this that the brain includes domain-general circuits that carry out the relevant mental operations. Instead, they hypothesize that language-selective and more general brain regions interact, whereby the general system carries out 'general operations on domain-specific knowledge representations' (Fedorenko and Shain 2021: 527). They claim that while language is specialized to certain areas of the brain, the mental operations themselves are not different from those in other domains of perception and cognition, as predicted by the cognitive commitment of Cognitive Grammar.

The cognitive commitment is an ontological statement about language in the mind and the brain, but it also encompasses a methodological imperative: when investigating a linguistic phenomenon, relate it to a general cognitive ability and see what this perspective has to offer. In our first case study, I will pursue this methodology and show that it leads to an insightful analysis of a complex sound change in the history of the Slavic languages. The second case study, which concerns morphosyntactic change in modern Russian, relates the cognitive commitment to social cognition.

## 2.2 Sound Change and Domain-General Cognitive Processes: The Case of the 'Jer Shift'

### 2.2.1 The Challenge

Few, if any, examples of language change have been more debated in Slavic linguistics than the so-called jer shift, a prosodic change that took place in Old

East Slavic in the twelfth century. The shift targeted two lax vowels, /ĭ, ŭ/, which are traditionally referred to as 'jers' or 'yers' in Slavic linguistics. The jers either disappeared or merged with /e, o/, depending on the prosodic environment. The challenge is to describe this environment in a principled and insightful way. The traditional approach is to count jers from right to left in the word, and assume that jers with odd numbers disappear, whereas jers with even numbers merge with non-jer vowels (Kiparsky 1963: 93). Imagine a sequence of three syllables where each vowel is a jer: $C\breve{U}_3C\breve{U}_2C\breve{U}_1$. Here, $\breve{U}$ represents a jer vowel. The subscripts represent the counting of jers from right to left. In such a sequence, the jers supplied with odd numbers (1 and 3) will disappear, while jer number 2 will turn into a non-jer vowel represented as O. In other words, we end up with the sequence CCOC. We may describe this as follows (Nesset 2016a: 579):

(5)     $C\breve{U}_3C\breve{U}_2C\breve{U}_1 \rightarrow$ CCOC, where C = consonant, $\breve{U}$ = lax vowel (jer: /ĭ, ŭ/), O=/o, e/

Here is an example (from Kiparsky 1963: 94), where jers number 1 and 3 disappear, while number 2 merges with /e/:[3]

(6)     $l\breve{i}_3st\breve{i}_2c\breve{i}_1 \rightarrow$ l'st'ec 'flatterer'

A complication occurs in words that contain both jers and non-jer vowels. Consider the following example (Kiparsky 1963: 94):

(7)     $ot\breve{u}_1xod\breve{i}_1niku \rightarrow$ otxodn'iku 'hermit (dative sg)'

This example shows that in order to predict the right outcome we are forced to restart the counting of jers after non-jer vowels. Thus, in (7) we assign the number '1' to the jer in the third syllable from the right, but since after that we encounter a non-jer vowel, we restart the counting of jers and thus assign the number '1' to the second jer as well. This enables us to predict the correct outcome, whereby both jers disappear.

The traditional approach can be summed up as follows (Nesset 2016a: 579):

(8)     a. Number consecutive jers from right to left.
        b. Restart the numbering from non-jer vowels.
        c. Jers with odd numbers are in weak position and disappear.
        d. Jers with even numbers are in strong position and vocalize to /e, o/.

While this is a good descriptive summary, its limitations are obvious. We know very little about what was going on in the minds of the speakers of Old East Slavic, but it is unlikely that they were counting jers from right to left. In other words, the statement in (8) is not psychologically realistic, and

---

[3] In this section, which focuses on phonology, examples are given in phonemic transcription. In the sections on morphosyntax, examples are rendered in transliterated orthography.

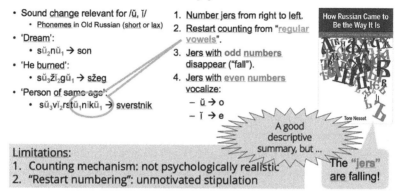

## Jer shift: Traditional approach

- Sound change relevant for /ŭ, ĭ/
  - Phonemes in Old Russian (short or lax)
- 'Dream':
  - sŭ₂nŭ₁ → son
- 'He burned':
  - sŭ₁žĭ₂gŭ₁ → sžeg
- 'Person of same age':
  - sŭ₃vĭ₂rstŭ₁nikŭ₁ → sverstnik

1. Number jers from right to left.
2. Restart counting from "regular vowels".
3. Jers with odd numbers disappear ("fall").
4. Jers with even numbers vocalize:
   - ŭ → o
   - ĭ → e

A good descriptive summary, but ...

The "jers" are falling!

How Russian Came to Be the Way It Is

Tore Nesset

Limitations:
1. Counting mechanism: not psychologically realistic
2. "Restart numbering": unmotivated stipulation

**Video 1** The traditional approach to the jer shift (video available at www.cambridge.org/nesset-resources)

therefore problematic from the point of view of the cognitive commitment. In addition, the statement in (8b) is an unmotivated stipulation. The advantages and limitations of the traditional approach are summarized in Video 1.

### 2.2.2 Rhythmic Grouping: Trochaic Feet

With the cognitive commitment in mind, we must ask whether it is possible to advance a psychologically realistic analysis that obviates the need for the stipulation in (8b). I argue that a more insightful analysis may be stated in terms of trochaic feet (i.e., rhythmic groups of two syllables where the leftmost syllable is prominent). A more detailed analysis is proposed in Nesset (2015: 246–51 and 2016c), but the following short summary is sufficient for present purposes:

(9)      a. Old East Slavic had trochaic feet.
         b. Feet were built from the right edge of the word.[4]
         c. A jer merges with a non-jer vowel if it is the head of a foot.
         d. All other jers disappear.

Consider the following string of consonants and jers, where parentheses mark feet:

(10)      CŬ(CŬCŬ) → CCVC

---

[4] For readers with little prior exposure to phonological theory it may seem unexpected that feet may be built from the right edge (i.e., the end of a word). However, this is not an unusual option in prosodic systems across the world (see, e.g., McCarthy and Prince 1993 and Kager 1999: 167).

As shown, this word contains one foot at the end of the word, and the only jer that merges with a non-jer vowel is the first jer inside the foot. The other jers disappear.

As we have seen, many words contain combinations of jers and non-jer vowels. How are feet built in such words? What is the inventory of legitimate feet in Old East Slavic? We may consider four logically possible combinations of jers and non-jers. I argue that three of them constitute legitimate feet:

(11)　　a. VŬ (e.g., *domŭ* 'house')
　　　　b. *ŬV (not attested)
　　　　c. ŬŬ (e.g., two last syllables in *lĭstĭcĭ* 'flatterer')
　　　　d. VV (e.g., two last syllables in *otŭxodĭniku* 'hermit (dative sg)')

The option in (11b) is marked with an asterisk, indicating that this is not a legitimate foot in Old East Slavic. This is not a mere stipulation but follows naturally from the assumption that Old East Slavic has trochaic feet. Recall that jers were lax, reduced vowels. It would be unnatural for such vowels to head a foot where the other syllable had an unreduced non-jer vowel. A foot of this type would be typologically marked since a reduced vowel would be in a prosodically more prominent position than an unreduced vowel. In a nutshell, I propose that a jer could only be the head of a foot if the other syllable also was a jer, as in (11c).

Let us now assign foot structure to the examples in (6) and (7):

(12)　　a. lĭ(stĭcĭ) → l'st'ec 'flatterer'
　　　　b. (otŭ)(xodĭ)(niku) → otxodn'iku 'hermit (dative sg)'

In (12a), we are able to build one foot, and we correctly predict that the jer that heads the foot merges with a non-jer vowel, while the remaining jers disappear. In (12b), we build three feet, and both jers disappear, since they are not heads of the relevant feet. Here is a more complicated example:

(13)　　(sŭžĭ)gla → sožgla 'she burned'

If we try to build a foot at the end of the word, the result would be an illegitimate foot of the *ŬV type. Therefore, we skip the last syllable of the word and build a foot on the remaining syllables. This allows us to correctly predict that the jer in the first syllable from the left merges with /o/, while the following jer disappears, since it is in a non-head position.

In section 2.2.1, I criticized the traditional account for involving an ad hoc stipulation, but is the alternative analysis in terms of trochaic feet any better? Example (12b) illustrates the difference between the two approaches.

According to the traditional approach, we would have to stipulate that we skip the full vowel between the jers before we start counting the jers anew (see (8b)). According to the trochee-based analysis, we can build trochaic feet without making any additional stipulations. This is a substantial improvement, since the analysis of examples like (12b) falls out as a natural consequence of a general theory about foot structure.

### 2.2.3 Rhythmic Organization and the Cognitive Commitment

Where does the cognitive commitment enter the picture? A similar trochee-based analysis could be couched in terms of, say, optimality theory or some other generative framework. However, the analysis I propose goes beyond descriptive elegance, since it illustrates the relevance of general cognitive mechanisms in historical linguistics. Feet are rhythmic groupings of syllables, and an analysis based on prosodic feet is psychologically realistic since rhythmic grouping is a fundamental property of human cognition (Ding et al. 2016). Nathan (2015: 266) writes that the rhythmic organization of prosodic properties 'simply is human rhythmic behaviour to which strings of segments are mapped, much as hand-clapping and foot-tapping is mapped to internally generated or externally perceived rhythms'. Rhythmic grouping of this kind is of critical importance in language acquisition; MacNeilage (2008: 108) demonstrates that infants' babbling, which represents an important step towards the acquisition of language, is inherently rhythmic 'from the very outset'. Moreover, this early rhythmic behaviour is not limited to language, but is rather part of a wide variety of repetitive body movements such as kicking, rocking, waving, bouncing, banging, rubbing, scratching, and swaying. Such repetitive body movements are characteristic of infants, and Thelen (1979) therefore calls them 'rhythmical stereotypies'. Rhythmic grouping is also important in music, and even if there are differences between the rhythmic organization of language and music (London 2012), there is a substantial body of evidence indicating that 'language and music may result from general perceptual mechanisms that are neither music- nor language-specific' (Goswami 2012: 60; see also Trehub and Hannon 2006 for discussion).

The upshot of this is that an analysis of the jer shift in terms of rhythmic grouping (i.e., trochaic feet) receives support from what we know about human cognition. By contrast, the traditional analysis in terms of an obscure counting procedure lacks any basis in human cognition. While an analysis in terms of trochees is psychologically plausible, the traditional counting mechanism is not.

Before we leave the jer shift, it is worth repeating that the analysis I have proposed illustrates that the cognitive commitment is more than an ontological statement about language in the mind and brain. As mentioned in Section 2.1, it is also a methodological imperative that forces us to look outside language when we analyse linguistic phenomena. This is exactly what we have done. Instead of analysing the jer shift in its own terms, we have connected it to a fundamental property of human cognition, viz. rhythmic grouping. The result is an elegant and insightful analysis. Clearly, the cognitive commitment has a lot to offer historical linguistics.

## 2.3 Social Cognition: Language Change as a Social and Mental Phenomenon and the Decade Construction Rivalry

### 2.3.1 Social Cognition

Is language a cognitive or a social phenomenon? Clearly, this is the wrong question to ask. It is both. Cognitive Grammar's cognitive commitment emphasizes the fact that language resides in the mind and brain of individual language users. However, this does not mean that Cognitive Grammar neglects the fact that language is also a 'social contract' in Saussure's (1983 [1916]: 25) terms (i.e., a cognitive phenomenon that is used for communication in a speech community). Langacker writes: '[C]ognitive linguistics stands out by emphasizing the semiological function of language. It fully acknowledges the grounding of language in social interaction, but insists that even its interactive function is critically dependent on conceptualization' (Langacker 2008: 7–8).

Although there is nothing in the fundamental assumptions of Cognitive Grammar that goes against the understanding of language as a social phenomenon, it may be fair to say that, in actual practice, the social dimension has not received as much attention in cognitive linguistics as it would deserve (Nesset 2016a: 574–5). However, recent years have witnessed a growing body of work bridging the gap between cognitive linguistics and sociolinguistics (cf., e.g., Geeraerts et al. 2010; Hilpert 2015: 357–9; Schmid 2015, 2020).

The notions of innovation and spread in historical linguistics illustrate how closely related the cognitive and social dimensions of language are. Traditionally, innovation and spread have been considered two distinct steps in language change. First, an innovation takes place in the mind of an individual language user (a cognitive phenomenon), and then the innovation spreads in the speech community (a social phenomenon). However, it may not be accurate to consider innovation a purely cognitive phenomenon, and it may be equally misleading to analyse spread as an exclusively social phenomenon, as pointed out by Schmid (2015: 12): 'If someone comes up with a witty and original new word and finds out that this word already exists [in the linguistic community], then they would no longer think of themselves as having produced an innovation'.

In other words, innovations presuppose linguistic conventions in a speech community, and innovation is therefore both a cognitive and a social phenomenon. The same goes for spread. Even if spread may be understood as a social process taking place in a speech community, the members of the speech community have minds. Therefore, it does not seem to be a particularly daring guess that spread depends on the cognitive abilities of the language users in the speech community (Nesset 2016a: 575).

Bybee (2021) takes this one step further and argues that innovation and spread are not necessarily distinct; according to her analysis, language change originates in the interplay between speaker and listener – what she refers to as 'joint innovation'. Given that the cognitive and social facets of language cannot be studied in isolation, it makes sense to investigate language change from the perspective of 'social cognition' (Diessel 2019: 25–27), that is, a perspective that seeks to integrate both cognitive and social aspects of language change. In the following case study, we will see how both aspects can be accommodated in a corpus study of ongoing change in temporal adverbials in Russian. However, first it is necessary to consider three synonymy avoidance strategies.

### *2.3.2 Three Ways to Avoid Synonymy*

It is well known in linguistics that complete synonymy is rare in language. Already in Saussure's *Cours* (1983 [1916]: 167) it was stated that 'inevitably the phonetic difference which has emerged will tend to acquire significance', which indicates that languages avoid complete synonymy. Among many others, Bloomfield (1933: 145), Nida (1958), Haiman (1980: 516) and Clark (1993: 2) make similar statements. In his textbook on lexical semantics, Cruse summarizes the situation as follows: '[O]ne thing becomes clear once we begin a serious quest for absolute synonyms, and that is that if they exist at all, they are extremely uncommon' (Cruse 1986: 270).

According to Goldberg (1995), synonymy avoidance is not restricted to lexical items. She argues that synonymous constructions are avoided (see also Bolinger 1968: 127):

(14)    The Principle of No Synonymy:
        'If two constructions are syntactically distinct, they must be semantically or pragmatically distinct'. (Goldberg 1995: 67)

For historical linguistics, this means that if complete synonymy 'were to occur, it would be unstable', as Cruse (1986: 270) aptly puts it. Three possible strategies for avoiding synonymy are conceivable (e.g., Croft 2000: 177–8; Szymanek 2005: 441; Blythe and Croft 2012: 278; Nuyts and Byloo 2015: 62–3; and Nesset and Makarova 2018: 73):

(15)     a.  Levelling: one form ousts its rival over time.
            b.  Sociolinguistic differentiation: the two rivals survive in different varieties of a language.
            c.  Semantic differentiation: the two rivals develop different meanings over time.

The three strategies are further described in Video 2, which emphasizes the interplay of cognitive and social factors.

It is important to notice that the three strategies in (15) are tightly intertwined. By way of illustration, consider the two Old Norse synonyms *ljúfr* and *kærr*, which both meant 'dear' (Bjorvand 2000: 325). The French borrowing *kærr* (cf. *cher*) ousted its rival in many varieties of Norwegian, but *ljúfr* has survived in some varieties, where it functions as a poetic word meaning 'wonderful' (see Hovdenak et al. 2001). In these varieties, we have sociolinguistic differentiation, since *ljufr* has become limited to poetic registers, and at the same time *ljufr* has changed its meaning from 'dear' to 'wonderful'. In other words, *ljufr* and *kærr* involve all three strategies at the same time: levelling, sociolinguistic differentiation, and semantic differentiation.

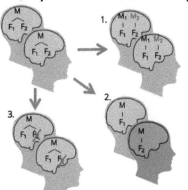

## Synonymy avoidance and diachrony:
## Mind, speech community, time

**Scenarios are not mutually exclusive!**

Three scenarios:

1. **Semantic differentiation:**
Forms develop different meanings.

2. **Socio-linguistic variation:**
Speakers develop different preferences.

3. **Levelling of form:**
One form ousts the other.

Research Question:
How can the *interplay* of factors be studied empirically?

**Video 2** The interplay of cognitive and social factors in language change – three scenarios (video available at www.cambridge.org/nesset-resources)

### 2.3.3 The Decade Construction Rivalry in Russian

Russian has two seemingly synonymous constructions that describe events taking place within a decade. In the following example, the preposition *v* 'in' is followed by an ordinal numeral and the word for 'year' in the locative (prepositional) case in the plural:[5]

(16)   **V**    **šestidesjat-yx**    **god-ax**       otec                eë      vernu-l-sja
       in     sixtieth-LOC.PL      year-LOC.PL     father[NOM.SG]      her     return-PST.M-REFL
       v      Moskv-u [. . .].
       in     Moscow-ACC.SG
       '**In the sixties**, her father returned to Moscow [. . .]' (Granin 1987)

However, in the following example, which also corresponds to *in the sixties*, the accusative case is used instead:

(17)   **V**    **šestidesjat-ye**    **god-y**        on         sozda-l          Cirk
       in     sixtieth-ACC.PL      year-ACC.PL     he[NOM]    create-PST.M     circus[ACC.SG]
       na     l'd-u.
       on     ice-LOC.SG
       '**In the sixties**, he created the Circus on ice.' (Kio 1995–9)

In Cognitive Grammar, the rivalry between the two Russian decade constructions can be analysed as a competition between two schemas in a category network. We will consider schemas in more detail in Section 3 and category networks in Section 4. For present purposes, it is sufficient to note that the two constructions represent a challenge to Goldberg's Principle of No Synonymy in (14). Since we would expect such situations to be unstable over time, the two constructions present an excellent test case for the three diachronic strategies discussed in the previous section: levelling, sociolinguistic differentiation, and semantic differentiation. In the following sections, we will investigate each strategy one at a time. For background information showing that both decade constructions are well motivated in the Russian grammar, see text box.

CASE MARKING IN RUSSIAN TEMPORAL ADVERBIALS – DOUBLE MOTIVATION

The variation between accusative and locative for decades is part of a bigger picture. For events that happen within a time span, Russian generally uses the preposition *v* 'in(to)' followed by an NP in the accusative case:

---

[5] In what follows, all numbered examples from Modern Russian are taken from the Russian National Corpus (www.ruscorora.ru).

(i)    Sluči-l-o-s'        **v**    **ètot**       **den'**       nesčast'-e
       happen-PST-N.SG-REFL   in   this[ACC.SG.M]   day[ACC.SG]   accident-NOM.SG
       **'On this day** an accident took place.' (Berezin 1998)

Here, the accident takes place at some point within the time span that is characterized as *ètot den'* 'this day'. However, for bounded time spans longer than a week, such as *god* 'year', *v* is normally followed by an NP in the locative case:

(ii)    **V**   **èt-om**      **god-u**       sluči-l-sja         rekordn-yj
       in   this-LOC.SG.M year-LOC.SG   happen-PST.SG.M-REFL   record-NOM.SG.M
       ulov.
       catch[NOM.SG]
       **'This year** saw a record high catch.' (Remneva 2009)

This rule only holds when the NP is in the singular. If we change *v ètom godu* 'this year' to *v èti gody* 'these years', the accusative is preferred:

(iii)    **V**        **èt-i**      **god-y**      Voznesensk-ij   išč-et
       in       this-ACC.PL   year-ACC.PL   V-NOM.SG.M    search-PST.3SG
       svo-ix     glavn-yx    gero-ev.
       his-ACC.PL   main-ACC.PL   hero-ACC.PL
       **'These years** Voznesenskij is looking for his main heros.' (Virabov 2015)

The accusative-locative variation for decades relates to the three rules illustrated in (i)–(iii). Decades are bounded time spans longer than a week, which leads us to expect the locative as in (ii). However, at the same time, the decades occur in the plural, which leads us to expect the accusative case as in (iii). The accusative is also the default case for temporal adverbials of the relevant type, as illustrated in (i). Therefore, the syntax of temporal adverbials in Russian offers motivation for the use of both cases in the decade constructions.

### 2.3.4 Levelling?

In order to find out if one of the rival constructions is in the process of ousting its competitor, Makarova and I created a database of 5,453 examples (2,670 examples with the accusative construction and 2,783 with the locative) from the Russian National Corpus. The examples span the period from 1830 to 2012, and since the corpus provides the year when each example was created, it is possible to investigate the competition of the two constructions over time. The relevant data are summarized in Table 2.

**Table 2** The distribution of the competing decade
constructions over time (raw numbers, adapted from Nesset
and Makarova 2018: 80)

|  | #Accusative | #Locative |
|---|---|---|
| 1826–50 | 1 | 17 |
| 1851–75 | 1 | 29 |
| 1876–1900 | 4 | 58 |
| 1901–25 | 14 | 77 |
| 1926–50 | 18 | 98 |
| 1951–75 | 154 | 220 |
| 1976–2000 | 356 | 241 |
| 2001–12 | 748 | 451 |
| Total (all periods) | 1,296 | 1,191 |

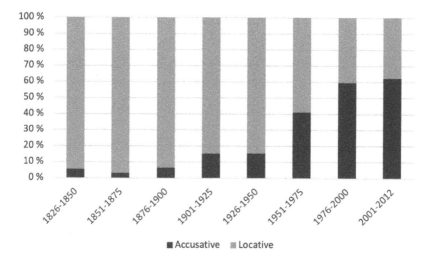

**Figure 1** The distribution of the competing decade constructions over time
(per cent, adapted from Nesset and Makarova 2018: 80)

Figure 1 shows that the locative construction dominated in the nineteenth
century, before the use of the accusative construction became more widespread
in the twentieth century. In the beginning of the twenty-first century, the
accusative is attested in more than 60 per cent of the relevant examples. Since
the accusative construction has strengthened its position over time, there is
some progress towards levelling, but at the same time the accusative has not
ousted its competitor completely, so the question arises as to whether sociolinguistic and semantic differentiation may also be relevant.

### 2.3.5 Sociolinguistic Differentiation?

Although the locative construction has been losing ground, it is still used in almost 40 per cent of the examples in the beginning of the twenty-first century. It is therefore relevant to ask whether the distribution of the two constructions to some extent depends on sociolinguistic variables. Which variables could be relevant? Regional variation? Social class? Potentially, there is no limit to which variables could be tested. Unfortunately, however, the available corpus resources are restricted. The Russian National Corpus enables us to investigate only two sociolinguistic variables, viz. genre and author gender.

In Nesset and Makarova (2018: 83–5), we considered three genres which we referred to as 'journalism', 'fiction', and 'scientific/educational'. The data are summarized in Table 3 and Figure 2.

As can be seen from the table and the figure, the three genres display very similar developments; for all three genres, the use of the accusative becomes more widespread over time, while the competing locative construction is losing ground. The differences in the dataset are not robust (Nesset and Makarova 2018: 84–5), so genre does not seem to be an important factor.

A similar conclusion can be drawn for the gender of the authors. For most examples, the corpus provides the name of the author, and on the basis of the name it is possible to establish the author's gender (Nesset and Makarova 2018: 85). Table 4 and Figure 3 summarize the situation. Since the differences are not robust, Makarova and I concluded that gender is not a relevant factor. Therefore, we do not have any evidence in favour of sociolinguistic differentiation, although it cannot be excluded that other sociolinguistic factors that we do not have access to may be relevant.

### 2.3.6 Semantic Differentiation?

In his widely used *A Comprehensive Grammar of Russian*, Wade (1992: 453) writes that 'with decades, the accusative is preferred for processes extending over a period', while 'the prepositional [locative] is preferred for an event occurring at a point within a decade'. In other words, Wade suggests that the two competing decade constructions are semantically differentiated, insofar as they are used with different kinds of events. Makarova and I tested this hypothesis in two ways but did not find any support for semantic differentiation.

First, we considered the grammatical aspect of the verb. As is well known, Russian has a grammaticalized distinction between perfective and imperfective verbs, whereby perfective verbs are typically used about completed events that take place at one point in time, while processes that extend over time and

**Table 3** The distribution of the competing decade constructions for three genres over time (raw numbers, adapted from Nesset and Makarova 2018: 84)

|  | **Journalism** |  | **Fiction** |  | **Scientific/Educational** |  |
| --- | --- | --- | --- | --- | --- | --- |
| Period | #Acc | #Loc | #Acc | #Loc | #Acc | #Loc |
| 1826–50 | 0 | 8 | 0 | 4 | 1 | 4 |
| 1851–75 | 1 | 15 | 0 | 7 | 0 | 7 |
| 1876–1900 | 4 | 34 | 0 | 15 | 0 | 5 |
| 1901–25 | 8 | 49 | 3 | 10 | 3 | 16 |
| 1926–50 | 9 | 45 | 2 | 18 | 6 | 32 |
| 1951–75 | 98 | 123 | 22 | 25 | 18 | 51 |
| 1976–2000 | 251 | 166 | 49 | 39 | 51 | 31 |
| 2001–12 | 582 | 330 | 32 | 19 | 122 | 89 |
| Total (all periods) | 953 | 770 | 108 | 137 | 201 | 235 |

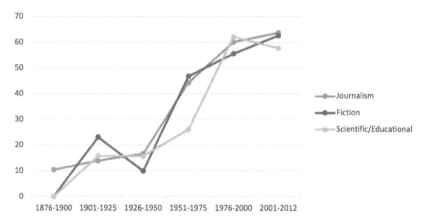

**Figure 2** The increased use of the accusative for three genres over time (per cent, adapted from Nesset and Makarova 2018: 84)

repeated events typically involve imperfective verbs. Arguably, therefore, Wade's hypothesis would predict that perfective verbs would prefer the locative construction, whereas the accusative construction would prevail for imperfective verbs. However, the data considered in Nesset and Makarova (2018: 91) did not offer any support for the relevance of the perfective/imperfective distinction for the rivalry between the accusative and locative cases in the decade constructions. Table 5 and Figure 4 indicate parallel developments for both aspects, and Makarova and I did not find any statistically robust differences.

In a second attempt to test Wade's hypothesis, Makarova and I carried out a more detailed classification of the events in each sentence. We distinguished

**Table 4** The distribution of the competing decade constructions for male and female authors over time (raw numbers, adapted from Nesset and Makarova 2018: 86). Periods refer to the time when the examples were created.

|  | **Male authors** | | **Female authors** | |
|---|---|---|---|---|
|  | #Acc | #Loc | #Acc | #Loc |
| 1801–25 | 2 | 29 | 0 | 3 |
| 1826–50 | 2 | 43 | 0 | 4 |
| 1851–75 | 15 | 69 | 0 | 7 |
| 1876–1900 | 24 | 72 | 5 | 7 |
| 1901–25 | 63 | 68 | 17 | 16 |
| 1926–50 | 127 | 78 | 15 | 10 |
| 1951–75 | 40 | 28 | 14 | 7 |
| Total (all periods) | 273 | 387 | 51 | 54 |

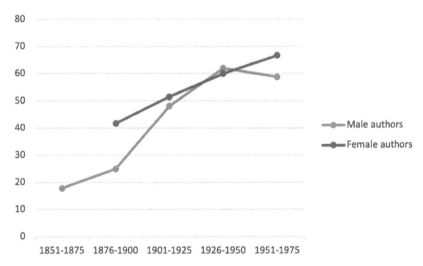

**Figure 3** The increased use of the accusative for male and female authors over time (per cent, adapted from Nesset and Makarova 2018: 86). Periods refer to the time when the examples were created.

between ten different types of events, including well-known categories such as accomplishments, activities, states, punctual events, and repeated events. However, even this detailed classification did not reveal any support for Wade's hypothesis, as we did not discover any robust statistical differences (Nesset and Makarova 2018: 95–6). In other words, our investigation did not find any indications of semantic differentiation. The story of the decade construction rivalry is mostly a story about levelling, not semantic or sociolinguistic differentiation.

**Table 5** The distribution of the competing decade constructions for perfective and imperfective verbs over time (raw numbers, adapted from Nesset and Makarova 2018: 91). Periods refer to the authors' year of birth.

|           | Perfective verbs | | Imperfective verbs | |
|-----------|------|------|------|------|
|           | #Acc | #Loc | #Acc | #Loc |
| 1801–25   | 1    | 15   | 1    | 16   |
| 1826–50   | 0    | 18   | 1    | 23   |
| 1851–75   | 5    | 37   | 7    | 26   |
| 1876–1900 | 10   | 35   | 12   | 32   |
| 1901–25   | 36   | 38   | 36   | 38   |
| 1926–50   | 75   | 48   | 56   | 66.7 |
| 1951–75   | 30   | 20   | 20   | 13   |
| Total     | 157  | 215  | 136  | 181  |

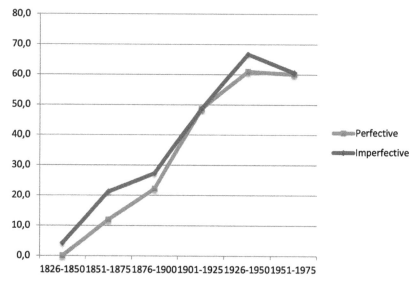

**Figure 4** The increased use of the accusative for perfective and imperfective verbs over time (per cent, adapted from Nesset and Makarova 2018: 86). Periods refer to the authors' year of birth.

I hasten to add that this conclusion is based on the available data – which are not ideal. With better corpus resources, we might have been able to provide a more fine-grained analysis of the interaction between levelling, semantic differentiation, and sociolinguistic differentiation.

## 2.4 Summing Up the Cognitive Commitment in Diachronic Linguistics

We have now explored two case studies that illustrate different aspects of Cognitive Grammar's cognitive commitment. The jer shift, a sound change in Old East Slavic, shows why it is advantageous to analyse language change in terms of general cognitive abilities. An analysis of the jer shift in terms of general rhythmic principles proved more insightful than the more traditional account based on a cognitively implausible counting procedure.

The second case study emphasizes that the cognitive commitment does not prevent us from considering the social aspects of language change. On the contrary, the cognitive and social aspects of change are intertwined. Although the story about the decades turned out to be mostly about levelling and not so much about sociolinguistic differentiation, the study demonstrates how both aspects can be incorporated in a corpus study of language change. At the same time, the decade construction rivalry illustrates the limitations of the available corpus resources. The theoretical concepts are in place and the methodology exists, but the corpus resources are not always up to the challenge.

## 3 The Semiotic Commitment: The Form/Meaning Bipolar Representation

Cognitive Grammar insists that language is all about conveying meaning. In two case studies about the semiotic commitment of Cognitive Grammar, we will see that this simple idea sharpens our understanding of language change. Section 3.2 concerns analogy in Russian verbs, while in Section 3.3 we turn to the emergence of new meaning in Russian numeral constructions. However, first it is necessary to clarify and contextualize the semiotic commitment.

### 3.1 What Is the Semiotic Commitment?

The semiotic commitment, which was introduced in Section 1.1, is the idea that Cognitive Grammar analyses language in terms of bipolar representations that connect form and meaning (and nothing else). This idea is part of a broader statement that Langacker refers to as the 'content requirement': 'The only structures permitted in the grammar of a language [...] are (1) phonological, semantic or symbolic structures that actually occur in linguistic expressions; (2) schemas for such structures; and (3) categorizing relationships involving the elements in (1) and (2)' (Langacker 1987: 53–4).

We will come back to the third part regarding categorizing relationships in Section 4, which is about the network commitment. The semiotic commitment is evident from parts 1 and 2 of the 'content requirement'. In this context, 'phonological structures' refer to linguistic form, that is, strings of sounds (in spoken languages) or handshapes etc. (in signed languages). 'Semantic structures' covers meaning in a broad sense (i.e., what is traditionally studied under the rubrics of semantics and pragmatics). Finally, symbolic structures are structures that connect form and meaning. Symbolic structures accommodate both morphological patterns (say, the structure of a word consisting of several morphemes) and syntactic constructions (say, the combination of a verb and a grammatical object in a certain case). Part 2 of the content requirement states that on the basis of language use, speakers make generalizations ('schemas') that concern form, meaning, or the relationship between form and meaning.

At first glance, this does not appear to be a particularly radical idea. After all, most linguists will probably subscribe to Saussure's (1983 [1916]: 97–103) idea that the sign – a combination of form and meaning – is of fundamental importance in language. What makes Langacker's content requirement radical is his insistence that phonological, semantic, and symbolic structures are the *only* permitted structures in a language. This does away with a considerable part of the machinery invoked by modern linguistics. Thus, in Cognitive Grammar there is no autonomous syntax, no arbitrary indices in morphological representations, and no abstract underlying phonological representations. Form and meaning – that is all there is in Cognitive Grammar.

The semiotic commitment (along with the rest of the content requirement) is a strong hypothesis about language that can be tested empirically. Imagine a situation where you encounter a linguistic phenomenon that cannot be analysed satisfactorily in terms of the structures licensed by the content requirement. In such a situation, you would have to give up and abandon the content requirement and the semiotic commitment. However, so far cognitive linguists have not experienced such situations, and the two case studies to be pursued in the following certainly suggest that the content requirement and the semiotic commitment are on the right track.

## 3.2 Analogy and Meaning: Two Changes in Russian Verbs

Analogy is one of the cornerstones of historical linguistics. Since analogy is a cognitive process, it has a natural place in a cognitive approach to language change. In what follows, we shall see that Cognitive Grammar's quest for meaning sharpens our insights about analogical change. We will explore the Semantic Homogeneity Constraint, which is a strong hypothesis stating that analogical change is restricted to semantically homogeneous domains. Juxtaposition of two changes in Russian verbs illustrate how this works.

## 3.2.1 Analogy: Asymmetry and Proximity

The term 'analogy' is traditionally used about change that is based on 'resemblance between the relationship of things rather than between the things themselves' (Anttila 1989: 105). A simple example from English may serve as an illustration. English has a relatively large class of strong verbs like *sing* which have a vowel alternation but no ending in the past tense: *sang*. A smaller class of verbs like *bring* has irregular past tense forms: *brought*. Some speakers regularize the past tense forms of *bring* to *brang* under the influence of the *sing-sang* relationship. One such speaker is my youngest stepdaughter, who as a teenager still insisted on using *brang* as the past tense form of *bring*. The traditional way of representing this is as follows (Anttila 1989: 89; Bybee 2015: 93–4):

(18)     *sing* : *sang* = *bring* : X
         X = *brang*

But under what conditions does analogical change take place? This is a fundamental question in historical linguistics. In Nesset and Makarova (2014), two conditions are discussed, which we refer to as 'asymmetry' and 'proximity'. The idea behind 'asymmetry' is that large classes have an impact on smaller classes.[6] In the case of English verbs, we have seen that the larger *sing* class exerts influence on the smaller class of *bring*. Other things being equal, we would not expect the smaller class to 'steal' members from the bigger class. The bigger classes generally get bigger, and in Nesset (2015: 84) I therefore use the term 'rich get richer' about the asymmetry condition.

The rationale behind the proximity condition is that analogical change is local. Joseph (2011: 405) uses the metaphor of a fog to explain this: '[S]peakers in the process of using – and thus of changing – their language often act as if they are in a fog, by which is meant not that they are befuddled but that they see clearly only immediately around them [...] they thus generalize only "locally"'. (Joseph 2011: 405)

In other words, analogical change takes place between words that are closely related, as in the case of *sing* and *bring* where both classes of verbs end in /ɪŋ/ in the infinitives and present tense (Bybee 2007a). However, what exactly does it mean to be 'closely related'? This is where Cognitive Grammar's semiotic commitment enters the picture. I suggest that analogical change takes place in

---

[6] Notice that there are a number of approaches in the literature on asymmetrical relationships based on the length of the forms (Mańczak's 1958 and 1980), markedness (Kuryłowicz 1995 [1949]), (type) frequency (Bybee 1985: 51; Bybee 2001, 2007a, 2007b), and informativeness (Albright 2008, 2009: 208–12). Detailed discussion of these approaches is beyond the scope of the present study.

semantically homogeneous domains. To see what that means, we will contrast
two examples of language change in Russian verbs.

### 3.2.2 Suffix Shift in Russian Verbs

Suffix shift is a typical example of analogical change in Russian verbs that has
received considerable attention in Russian linguistics (e.g., Gorbačevič 1978;
Andersen 1980; Comrie, Stone, and Polinsky 1996; Graudina et al. 2001;
Gagarina 2003; Gor and Chernigovskaya 2004 and 2005; Gor 2007; Janda,
Nesset, and Baayen 2010; Nesset 2010; Nesset and Kuznetzova 2011).
Although many facets of the phenomenon have been debated, the basic facts
are uncontroversial. Russian has a large and productive class of verbs like *delat'*
'do' and a smaller class of verbs like *kapat'* 'drip', and the larger class attracts
members from the smaller class. Compare the inflectional paradigms of the two
types of verbs in Table 6, where the forms of *kapat'* are the archaic forms that
reflect the situation before analogical change.

Analogical change takes place, whereby verbs like *kapat'* adopt the same
inflection as the *delat'* class. Instead of traditional present tense forms like *kaplet*
(phonemically /kapʲot/) 'drip (3 Sg present) are replaced by new present tense
forms like *kapaet* (/kapajot/), which resemble *delaet* (/delajot/) 'do (3 sg present).
In the tradition of Jakobson (1948), the *kapat'* class is said to involve the verb
suffix *-a*, while the *delat'* class has the suffix *-aj*. This is why the analogical change
is referred to as 'suffix shift': the *kapat'* class shifts from one suffix to another.

If we consider suffix shift from the perspective of asymmetry and proximity,
it becomes clear that both conditions are met. We are dealing with verbs that
migrate from a small class under the influence of a large and productive class of
verbs, so the relation between the two classes is clearly asymmetrical in the
relevant sense. With regard to the proximity condition, the two classes are also
closely related, since, as shown from the paradigms in Table 6, both classes of
verbs are inflected in the same way in the past tense and infinitive forms. In
other words, the two classes share a part of their inflectional paradigms.[7] On the
basis of this similarity, the present tense and imperative forms of the smaller
class undergo change and the verbs adopt present tense and imperative forms of
the type found in the larger class. This is shown in Video 3.

---

[7] As pointed out by an anonymous reviewer, the two verb classes illustrate that the proximity
principle goes beyond mere phonological similarity (as in *sing* and *bring*). What creates the
proximity between the two verb classes is the fact that they share parts of their inflectional
paradigms, which involve both form (certain endings) and meaning (certain inflectional features
such as past tense).

**Table 6** The inflection of *kapat'* 'drip' and *delat'* 'do' (phonemic transcription, suffixes separated by means of hyphens)

|  | Unproductive | Productive |
|---|---|---|
| 3 sg non-past | kaplʲ-ot | dʲel-aj-ot |
| 3 pl non-past | kaplʲ-ut | dʲel-aj-ut |
| Imperative sg | kaplʲ-i | dʲel-aj |
| Imperfective gerund | kaplʲ-a | dʲel-aj-a |
| Masculine sg past | kap-a-l | dʲel-a-l |
| Feminine sg past | kap-a-l-a | dʲel-a-l-a |
| Pl past | kap-a-lʲ-i | dʲel-a-lʲ-i |
| Infinitive | kap-a-tʲ | dʲel-a-tʲ |

## Suffix shift: Asymmetry & Proximity

| | Unproductive | | PRODUCTIVE | |
|---|---|---|---|---|
| 3 sg present | kaplʲ-ot | kap-aj-ot | dʲel-aj-ot | Asymmetry: "Rich get richer" |
| 3 pl present | kaplʲ-ut | kap-aj-ut | dʲel-aj-ut | |
| Imperative | kaplʲ-i | kap-aj | dʲel-aj | |
| Active participle | kaplʲ-uʃ-ij | kap-aj-uʃ-ij | dʲel-aj-uʃ-ij | |
| Gerund | kaplʲ-a | kap-aj-a | dʲel-aj-a | |
| Masc. sg past | kap-a-l | | dʲel-a-l | Proximity: Partial overlap |
| Pl past | kap-a-lʲ-i | | dʲel-a-lʲ-i | |
| Infinitive | kap-a-tʲ | | dʲel-a-tʲ | |

**Result: VARIATION and gradual shift to -aj**

**Asymmetry:** Unproductive (small) vs. productive (large) class
**Proximity:** Partially overlapping paradigms
**Prediction:** Verbs move from unproductive to productive pattern
✓ Prediction is borne out by the facts!

**Video 3** Suffix shift as an example of analogical change – asymmetry and proximity (video available at www.cambridge.org/nesset-resources)

### 3.2.3 Two Types of Russian Verbs in -nu

In order to clarify the relevance of Cognitive Grammar's semiotic commitment, we may contrast suffix shift with the diachronic development of Russian verbs in *-nu*. Once again, we are dealing with two classes of verbs. A relatively small class displays a /nu/~Ø ('zero') alternation, whereby the *-nu* suffix is dropped in the past tense.[8] In Table 7, *privyknut'* 'become used to' illustrates this. The inflection of *privyknut'* is compared to *maxnut'* 'wave', which represents a class of verbs expressing so-called semelfactive aktionsart. We will return to the semelfactive verbs in Section 4.2. For present purposes, it is sufficient to

---

[8] The Ø symbol is used for descriptive convenience. No claims are made about 'zero morphs'. See, for example, Anderson 1992: 61 and Nesset 1998: 79–82 for discussion.

**Table 7** The inflection of verbs in *-nu*: unproductive and productive classes (phonemic transcription, suffixes separated by means of hyphens, Ø represents the absence of a suffix)

|  | **Unproductive** | **Productive** |
|---|---|---|
| 3 sg non-past | prʲivik-nʲ-ot | max-nʲ-ot |
| 3 pl non-past | prʲivik-n-ut | max-n-ut |
| Imperative sg | prʲivik-nʲ-i | max-nʲ-i |
| Masculine sg past | prʲivik-Ø | max-nu-l |
| Feminine sg past | prʲivik-Ø-l-a | max-nu-l-a |
| Pl past | prʲivik-Ø-lʲ-i | max-nu-lʲ-i |
| Past active participle | prʲivik-Ø-ş-ij | max-nu-vş-ij |
| Perfective gerund | prʲivik-Ø-şi | max-nu-v |
| Infinitive | prʲivik-nu-tʲ | max-nu-tʲ |

acknowledge two facts about the semelfactive verbs. Unlike verbs like *privyknut'*, semelfactives constitute a large and productive class, and the semelfactive verbs preserve *-nu* throughout the paradigm.

As depicted in Table 7, the situation is neat and simple, but in actual practice things are more complicated. The rule that verbs like *privyknut'* drop the *-nu* suffix in the past tense is not obligatory, and alternative past tense forms like *privyknul* (masculine singular past tense) that preserve *-nu* are attested. On the face of it, this looks like an analogical change that meets both the asymmetry and proximity conditions. We are dealing with an asymmetrical relationship between a large and a small class, and the two classes are similar insofar as they are inflected in the same way in the present tense and the imperative. Both classes furthermore display the *-nu* suffix in the infinitive. Against this background, we would expect analogical change to take place and the use of past tense forms in *-nu* to increase over time for verbs like *privyknut'*. However, as we will see in the next section, this prediction is not borne out by the facts – and the semiotic commitment of Cognitive Grammar helps us understand why.

### 3.2.4 The Semantic Homogeneity Constraint

Figure 5 juxtaposes the development of suffix shift with that of the verbs with *-nu*. Both curves represent the suffixes of the productive classes, which we expect to increase in use as the result of analogical change. For suffix shift, represented as a blue line in the figure, the prediction is borne out. Admittedly, we are not dealing with a steep increase and there is a dip in the twentieth century before the use of *-aj* goes up in the twenty-first century. This has to do

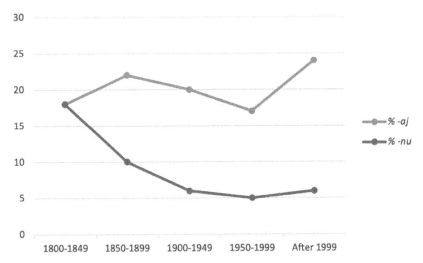

**Figure 5** Suffix shift and verbs with *-nu* – development of the productive suffixes

with the fact that there are individual differences among verbs (in part, at least, related to the sound shape of their stems, Nesset 2010). It has furthermore been shown that there are differences among the inflectional forms; some forms are more likely to adopt the productive suffix, while other forms are more resistant to analogical change (Janda et al. 2010). However, these details need not concern us here, since as pointed out by Andersen (1980: 297), the synchronic situation of the relevant verbs 'has all the earmarks of a change in progress'. Things may not be changing fast, but analogical change is in progress.

The development of verbs in *-nu* goes in the opposite direction, as shown by the red line in Figure 5. From the perspective of analogical change, we would expect the productive pattern to gradually take over (i.e., for the use of *-nu* to increase in the past tense forms of verbs like *privyknut'*). But this is not what is happening. Instead, the use of *-nu decreases* over time.

The question now arises as to why analogical change takes place in the case of suffix shift, but not for verbs in *-nu*. On the face of it, the two cases seem entirely parallel, but they nevertheless behave differently. I propose that the semiotic commitment of Cognitive Grammar offers a principled explanation.

So far, we have not considered the *meaning* of the suffixes in question. For suffix shift, there is not much to say. The *-a* and *-aj* suffixes are derivational suffixes that signal that the relevant words are verbs. In view of the semiotic commitment, we may follow Langacker, who argues for semantic definitions of parts of speech in Cognitive Grammar (Langacker 2008: 93–127). The meaning of -*a* and -*aj* is therefore to signal verbhood. While the details of Langacker's argument are not important here, it is crucial that there is no clear semantic difference between the two suffixes. They are both ways of signalling that the relevant word is a verb.

For the verbs in -*nu*, on the other hand, we are dealing with two suffixes with different meanings. As mentioned in Section 3.2.3, the productive class of verbs with -*nu* is commonly referred to as 'semelfactive verbs'. We will return to a more detailed discussion of the term 'semelfactive' in Section 4.2. For now, it is sufficient to say that the semelfactive -*nu* suffix means that the relevant action is carried out once. *Maxnut'*, for instance, may be glossed as 'wave once', since it implies that a single wave takes place.

It is less straightforward to identify the meaning of -*nu* in the unproductive class. The traditional label 'inchoative' is sometimes used (cf., e.g., Schuyt 1990), but Padučeva (1996: 117) prefers the term 'gradative' (Russian: *gradativ*), since verbs like *soxnut'* 'become dry' strictly speaking do not denote the beginning of a process. Be that as it may, it is clear that -*nu* in the unproductive class has a different meaning than the semelfactive -*nu* of the productive class.

Cognitive Grammar's semiotic commitment forces us to take the meaning of grammatical morphemes seriously, and this enables us to identify the difference between suffix shift (where the relevant suffixes have the same meaning and analogical change takes place) and verbs in -*nu* (where the suffixes have different meanings and analogical change does not take place). In Nesset and Makarova (2014), we proposed the following constraint on analogical change:

(19)    Semantic Homogeneity Constraint:
        Analogical change is restricted to semantically homogeneous domains.

What this means is that analogical change can affect affixes with the same meaning, such as -*a* and -*aj* involved in suffix shift, while analogical change does not take place for affixes with different meanings, such as -*nu* in the semelfactive and non-semelfactive verb classes. Semantic differences of the kind we observe in verbs with -*nu* represent barriers that may block analogical change. The Semantic Homogeneity Constraint may be considered a hypothesis that can be tested in future research. In this way, it illustrates how Cognitive Grammar's semiotic commitment leads us to advance new hypotheses that sharpen our understanding of analogical change.

### 3.2.5 An Apparent Exception

Before we leave the verbs in *-nu*, we must consider an apparent exception, which, however, upon closer inspection lends additional support to the Semantic Homogeneity Constraint. Figure 5 in the previous section shows that the use of *-nu* has decreased in general. However, different inflectional forms behave differently. While, as shown in Figure 6, for most forms the use of *-nu* is low and/or decreasing, the non-finite forms (gerund and participles) display the opposite tendency (Graudina, Ickovič and Katlinskaja 2001).[9] The question is: why does the use of *-nu* increase for non-finite forms?

If we interpret the increasing use of *-nu* as the result of analogy to the semelfactive verbs, we go against the Semantic Homogeneity Constraint, since we would have to accept analogical change despite the semantic differences between the productive and unproductive classes of verbs in *-nu*. Do the non-finite forms force us to give up the Semantic Homogeneity Constraint?

I argue that the answer is 'no'. Instead, I propose a different account, which arguably supports the constraint. If the behaviour of the non-finite forms were due to the influence of semelfactive verbs, we would not be able to explain why the change targets non-finite forms. Instead, we would expect all inflected forms to be equally likely targets of analogical change, since semelfactive verbs display the *-nu* suffix in all inflected forms.

As an alternative explanation, I therefore suggest that it is the infinitive of the verbs in the non-productive class that is the source of analogical change. Recall that the infinitive always keeps the *-nu* suffix. This is a likely source of analogy, since the infinitive is a non-finite form that is closely related to participles and gerunds, and since the three forms generally share the same stem in Russian verbs.[10] In short, I propose that infinitives, participles, and gerunds constitute a semantically homogeneous domain, where analogical change is likely to take place.[11] Although this account is somewhat speculative, it shows that the behaviour of non-finite forms may not be at variance with the Semantic Homogeneity Constraint, but instead lends additional support to the proposed constraint.

---

[9] As shown in Figure 6, there is one deviation from this pattern, which concerns prefixed active participles. For discussion, see Nesset and Makarova (2012: 52).

[10] As an anonymous reviewer points out, there are some exceptions to this generalization. An example where participles group with finite forms is *umeret'* 'die', insofar as the participle *umeršij* and the finite past tense form *umer* share the same stem.

[11] I will not discuss the non-trivial issue concerning the semantic properties underlying the distinction between finite and non-finite verb forms in Russian. Arguably, finite forms express mood, while non-finite forms do not. Furthermore, participles and infinitives have syntactic properties that resemble those of adjectives and nouns, which set these forms apart from finite verb forms. In view of Langacker's 'content requirement', both morphological categories like mood and parts of speech can be defined in semantic terms (see discussion in Langacker 2008: 93–128 and 259–309).

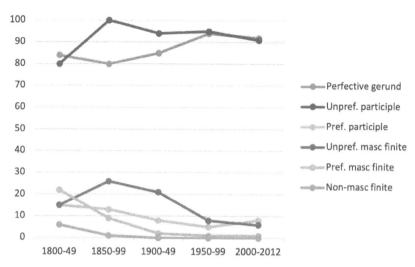

**Figure 6** Development of *-nu* in past tense forms of unprefixed and prefixed verbs, adapted from Nesset and Makarova 2014: 179

### 3.2.6 Summing Up

Cognitive Grammar's semiotic commitment forces us to take meaning seriously and thus sharpens our understanding of analogy. Analogical change is predicted to take place within semantically homogeneous domains, but not for linguistic items with different meanings. The Semantic Homogeneity Constraint is a hypothesis that can be tested in future research on language change.

## 3.3 When a Form Acquires a New Meaning: Reanalysis and the Emerging Feminine Numeral Construction

The semiotic commitment implies a strong focus on the meaning of grammatical constructions. Although there are many differences between words and grammatical morphemes, Langacker insists that grammatical morphemes express meaning essentially in the same way as words do. In view of this, an important task for a historical linguist working within Cognitive Grammar is to study changes in the meaning of grammatical constructions. In the following, we will consider numeral constructions in Russian, which arguably are in the process of acquiring a new meaning.

### 3.3.1 The Problem

In modern Russian, 'two new apartments' can be expressed in two different ways:

(20) Dv-e       nov-yx        kvartir-y
two-F.NOM   new-GEN.PL   apartment-GEN.SG
'Two new apartments'

(21) Dv-e       nov-ye   kvartir-y
two-F.NOM   new-??   apartment-GEN.SG
'Two new apartments'

In both examples, the numeral and noun have the same forms, but the adjective displays different endings, *-yx* in (20) and *-ye* in (21). The *-yx* ending represents the genitive plural; Nominative forms of Russian numerals generally govern the genitive case, and in numeral constructions adjectives generally occur in the plural, so the genitive plural ending *-yx* is what we would expect. However, it is far from obvious what the *-ye* ending conveys. Is it a nominative plural ending? Or is it a marker of another case or number (e.g., a 'numerative' case) or a 'paucal' number (i.e., a special form related to the numerals 2, 3, and 4)? The term 'paucal' is traditionally used in Russian linguistics about the numerals 2, 3, and 4, whose morphosyntax is quite complex, as shown in the text box below. We will consider the *-ye* ending in Section 3.3.4, where I will argue that it is a marker of feminine gender. In (21), the ending is glossed as ?? to highlight the fact that its meaning is controversial.

COMPLEXITY: THE MORPHOSYNTAX OF RUSSIAN NUMERALS IN A NUTSHELL

The changes in the paucal constructions are part of an extensive restructuring of the Russian numerals, which started with the disappearance of the dual number in medieval times. The following example illustrates the complexity of the resulting system:

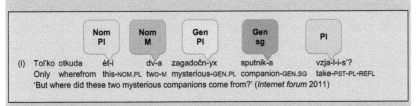

(i) Tol'ko otkuda   èt-i     dv-a  zagadočn-yx   sputnik-a       vzja-l-i-s'?
Only  wherefrom  this-NOM.PL  two-M  mysterious-GEN.PL  companion-GEN.SG  take-PST-PL-REFL
'But where did these two mysterious companions come from?' (*Internet forum* 2011)

As shown, all the inflected words in the construction involve different and partially conflicting sets of morphosyntactic features – a truly complex system!

Before we go on, it is necessary to discuss the grammatical features of the numeral and noun involved in the construction and clarify the relevance of the semiotic commitment. The numeral has the ending -*e*, which signals nominative case and feminine gender. The fact that -*e* represents the nominative is evident from comparison with oblique cases that have the endings -*ux* (genitive and locative), -*um* (dative), and -*umja* (instrumental).[12] It is also uncontroversial that the ending -*e* in *dve* marks feminine gender, since the ending is used when the numeral combines with feminine nouns such as *kvartira* 'apartment' in (20) and (21). In constructions with masculine or neuter nouns, the numeral has the ending -*a*, as in *dva stola* 'two tables' (with the masculine noun *stol* 'table') and *dva okna* 'two windows' (with the neuter noun *okno* 'window').

The situation for the noun is less obvious, since feminine nouns like *kvartira* 'apartment' have the ending -*y* in the genitive singular and the nominative plural. Is the noun in the genitive singular or the nominative plural in examples like (20) and (21)? A number of different analyses have been discussed in the copious scholarly literature on Russian numeral syntax (see, e.g., Zaliznjak 2002 [1967]; Mel'čuk 1985; Corbett 1993; Andersen 2006; Pereltsvaig 2010; Igartua and Madariaga 2018). While the ending is ambiguous, stress patterns offer an empirical argument in favour of the genitive singular. Russian has a class of nouns which display different stress placement in the singular and the plural. A case in point is *ruká* 'hand, arm', which carries stress on the ending in the singular, but on the stem in the plural. Thus, the genitive singular is *rukí*, while the nominative plural is *rúki*. In numeral constructions, the form with end stress is used: *dve rukí* 'two hands/arms' (see Nesset and Nordrum 2019 for discussion and references). In other words, we are dealing with the genitive singular, not the nominative plural.

At this point, the reader may ask whether the categories of case and gender represent *meaning*. In view of the semiotic commitment, which insists that grammatical endings convey meaning, we are forced to connect traditional grammatical categories with meaning. While detailed discussion of case and gender is beyond the scope of the present study, a couple of general points are in order. First, Cognitive Grammar's quest for meaning in grammar is by no means new. In Slavic linguistics, Jakobson's (1936) discussion of invariant meanings of the Russian cases is a good example (see also Worth 1984). However, as

---

[12] The accusative case involves an additional complication since it is syncretic with the nominative in constructions with inanimate nouns and with the genitive for animate nouns. I will not discuss this syncretism pattern since it is not relevant for the problem under scrutiny.

pointed out by Wierzbicka (1980) the invariant meanings that have been postulated tend to be quite abstract and have limited predictive power. In view of this, cognitive linguists have instead represented the meanings of the Russian cases as networks of less abstract meanings. For instance, Janda and Clancy (2002: 111) analyse the meaning of the Russian genitive as a network with four schemas: SOURCE, GOAL, WHOLE, and REFERENCE.

It is also possible to analyse gender in terms of networks structured around semantically defined prototypes. Corbett (1991: 8) has claimed that all known grammatical gender systems in the languages of the world have a semantic core related to biological gender or some other semantic distinction. In view of this, it would be feasible to analyse the Russian genders as networks structured around the prototypes of male and female biological gender. Phillips and Boroditsky (2003) have argued that semantics is relevant even for the gender of nouns that do not refer to male or female humans or animals.

Now that we have seen how the semiotic commitment forces us to analyse grammatical categories in semantic terms, we are ready to consider the *-ye* ending of the adjective in example (21). However, before we turn to this problem in Sections 3.3.3 and 3.3.4, it must be shown that the rivalry between the *-yx* and *-ye* endings in (20) and (21) is part of an ongoing language change.

### 3.3.2 Diachronic Development

In Nesset (2020), I studied a dataset of approximately 6,000 examples from the Russian National Corpus. The dataset covers constructions with the 'paucal' numerals *dva/dve* 'two', *tri* 'three' and *četyre* 'four' followed by an adjective and a noun. The study clearly indicates that we are dealing with language change, as shown in Figure 7.

The examples were divided into twenty-five-year periods covering the time span from 1825 to 2015. The three curves in the figure show the development for constructions involving nouns of different grammatical genders. As shown, before 1850 the *-yx* ending was used in less than 30 per cent of examples for all three genders. Then the use of *-yx* gradually became more widespread, until it established itself as the general rule for all genders in the middle of the twentieth century. At this point a split took place, while the use of *-yx* continued to increase for masculine and neuter nouns, feminine nouns showed the opposite development. As a result, in the twenty-first century, *-yx* has become a nearly categorical rule for masculine and neuter nouns. For feminine nouns, on the other hand, *-ye* has established itself as the dominant suffix which is now used in

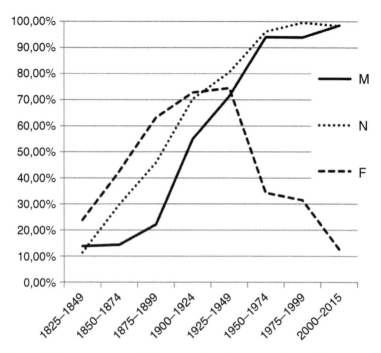

**Figure 7** The percentage of the *-yx* ending in constructions with a paucal numeral followed by an adjective and a masculine, feminine or neuter noun

nearly 90 per cent of the examples in the most recent period. We observe a clear division of labour between the two endings. For masculine and neuter nouns, *-yx* is used, whereas *-ye* is the preferred choice for feminine nouns.

### 3.3.3 The Bigger Picture

Before we go on to consider the meaning of the *-ye* ending, it is important to understand that the diachronic development shown in Figure 7 is part of a bigger picture, whereby gender-specific constructions have gradually developed. This development started in the Middle Ages, when Old East Slavic lost the dual number (see Žolobov 2002, Nesset 2020: 517–18 for discussion). This led to a restructuring of constructions with paucal numerals. While the details of the development are debated in Slavic linguistics, a brief outline of some major facts is sufficient for present purposes.

The first thing that happened was a redistribution of the division of labour between *dva* and *dve*. Originally, the ancestor of today's *dve* was used with neuter and feminine nouns, but neuter nouns gradually migrated towards the ancestor of today's form *dva*. In other words, the numeral *dve* became a marker of feminine gender, while *dva* was used with nouns of masculine and neuter. This development appears to have been completed by the eighteenth century (Kiparsky 1967: 174).

The endings of the nouns also underwent change. Gradually the -*y* ending came to dominate for nouns of feminine gender, while for masculine and neuter nouns the ending -*a* established itself as the general rule. This change was in place by the eighteenth century (Žolobov 2002). The result was feminine constructions with *dve* followed by a feminine noun in -*y* (e.g., *dve kvartiry* 'two apartments') and masculine and neuter constructions with *dva* followed by nouns ending in -*a*, such as *dva stola* 'two tables' and *dva okna* 'two windows'.

The changes in the numeral and nouns set the stage for the changes in the adjectives, explored in the previous section. As we have seen, in the nineteenth century there was extensive variation, but in the twentieth century the -*yx* ending became the rule for masculine and neuter nouns, before -*ye* established itself as the dominant ending for feminine nouns in the beginning of the twenty-first century. The developments are summarized in Table 8. As shown, the changes in the distribution of the adjective endings represent the last stage in a long chain of changes, which have resulted in the development of gender-specific constructions with paucal numerals. For an illustration, see Video 4.

Table 8 illustrates the advantages of Cognitive Grammar's semiotic commitment. The strong emphasis on meaning enables us to identify a common denominator for the changes summarized in the table, viz., the expression of feminine gender.

### 3.3.4 The Emergence of a New Meaning

Let us now turn to the question we started with: what is the meaning of the -*ye* ending? We start with an example without a numeral:

(22)     Sil'n-ye              rúk-i
         strong-NOM.PL        arm-NOM.PL
         'Strong hands/arms (nominative plural)'

In Russian, adjectives agree with the noun they modify. Agreement can be defined as 'systematic covariance between a semantic or formal property of one element and a formal property of another' (Steele 1978: 610; Corbett 2006: 4). In other words, we expect the adjective to have features that are compatible with the features of the noun. In the simple

**Table 8** The development of gender-specific constructions with paucal numerals

| Century | Part of speech | Language change |
|---------|----------------|-----------------|
| By 18th | Numeral | *Dve* used exclusively with feminine nouns |
| By 18th | Noun | Ending *-y* used exclusively on feminine nouns |
| 19th | Adjective | Variation between *-yx* and *-ye* for all genders |
| 20th | Adjective | Ending *-yx* becomes the rule for masculine/neuter gender |
| 21st | Adjective | Ending *-ye* becomes dominant for feminine gender |

# Development of gender-specific constructions

- The paucal constructions include
  - Numeral + adjective + noun
  - 'two new apartments'
- Numeral:
  - Separate feminine form *dve* 'two' in place before 18th century
- Noun:
  - Separate feminine form (*-y*) in place before 18th century
- Adjective:
  - 19th century: variation
  - 20th century: *-ye* disappears for MN
  - 21st century: *-yx* disappears for F

The association of adj and gender is the last stage in the birth of gender-specific paucal (sub)constructions!

A truly long birth for a construction!

**Video 4** The development of gender-specific constructions with paucal numerals numerals (video available at www.cambridge.org/nesset-resources)

example (22), this is indeed the case. The noun is in the nominative plural, and the *-ye* ending of the adjective marks the same features. This becomes clear if we replace the nominative plural form *rúki* with, say, the genitive singular *rukí* (with stress on the ending). If we want to combine the adjective with the genitive singular form of the noun, we are forced to use the ending *-oj* instead of *-ye*.

(23)    Sil'n-oj            ruk-í
        strong-F.GEN.SG     arm-GEN.SG
        'Strong hand/arm (genitive singular)'

If you hear someone say *sil'nye*, you have reasons to expect a noun in the nominative plural afterwards, while *sil'noj* will trigger other expectations.

With this in mind, we may consider the more complex example with a numeral:

(24) Dv-e       sil'n-ye   ruk-í
     two-F.NOM   new-F      apartment-GEN.SG
     'Two strong hands/arms'

It is tempting to suggest that *-ye* is a marker of nominative plural in the same way as in example (22), but an analysis along those lines would imply a feature clash, since the following noun is in the genitive singular. Instead, we must ask: what does the adjectival ending convey? If you hear the string *dve sil'nye*, you can be absolutely sure that the following noun will be of feminine gender, since in present-day Russian only feminine nouns combine with a paucal numeral followed by an adjective in *-ye*. Admittedly, the numeral *dve* alone is sufficient to show that the noun will be feminine, since *dve* is opposed to the masculine and neuter form *dva*. However, even in constructions with *tri* 'three', which does not have a separate feminine form, the string *tri sil'nye* is sufficient to determine that the following noun will be feminine. In this sense, *-ye* can be analysed as a marker of feminine gender, as shown in the Leipzig glossing in (24).

A strong argument in favour of this analysis is the diachronic development discussed in the previous sections. The changes in the numeral, noun and adjective all have one thing in common – they emphasize the difference between feminine nouns on the one hand and masculine and neuter nouns on the other.

A possible disadvantage with the proposed analysis is that it involves homonymy. In examples like (22) without a numeral, *-ye* is a marker of nominative and plural, while in constructions with a paucal numeral, the ending signals feminine gender. However, this is not a very strong objection since many other endings signal different meanings in different constructions. A case in point is the *-oj* ending in (23), which is used in the genitive, dative, instrumental, and locative singular of Russian adjectives. Another example is the adjectival ending *-yx*, which may signal both genitive and locative plural. In other words, endings with multiple meanings are widespread, and it is therefore not unexpected that *-ye* may convey more than one meaning.

It is worth pointing out that the analysis I propose leaves open the important question as to whether *-ye* in addition to feminine gender also marks case and/or number. It has been suggested that constructions with paucal numerals involve a numerative case (Zaliznjak 2002 [1967]) or a paucal number (Corbett 1993;

Pereltsvaig 2010; Igartua and Madariaga 2018). These analyses are not at variance with the analysis I have presented here, since Russian adjectives are inflected for gender, number, and case, and have endings that mark different combinations of features for the three categories. However, a detailed discussion of number and case is beyond the scope of the present study.

## 3.4 Summing Up the Semiotic Commitment in Diachronic Linguistics

Two conclusions emerge from our discussion of Cognitive Grammar's semiotic commitment. First, the semiotic commitment implies a strong emphasis on meaning that sharpens our understanding of a fundamental concept in historical linguistics, namely analogy. We have explored the Semantic Homogeneity Constraint, which represents a strong hypothesis about the semantic conditions that must be met in order for analogical change to take place. The constraint yields correct predictions for important changes in Russian verbs and has the potential to inform future research on analogical change.

The second conclusion regards the analysis of numeral constructions. We have seen that the semiotic commitment forces us to consider the meaning of grammatical morphemes, and that this enables us to identify a common denominator for a series of changes, which yield different paucal constructions for feminine nouns on the one hand and masculine and neuter nouns on the other. The semiotic commitment furthermore inspires us to rethink the meaning of the adjective ending in the feminine paucal construction, and thus sheds new light on a contested issue in Russian linguistics.

## 4 The Network Commitment: Language as a 'Constructicon'

'Everything is related to everything', is a famous statement made by Gro Harlem Brundtland, Norway's first female prime minister and director-general of the World Health Organization.[13] Ms Brundtland's remark was about politics, but her insight certainly concerns language as well. As conceptualized in Cognitive Grammar, language is a large network where everything is related to everything. In this section, we will turn to the network commitment and explore how this commitment facilitates an insightful analysis of the emergence and development of the semelfactive category in Russian. Section 4.1 details the relevant theoretical assumptions, before we consider the semelfactive verbs in Section 4.2. Section 4.3 summarizes the contribution of category networks in diachronic linguistics.

---

[13] The wording in Norwegian is 'alt henger sammen med alt'. The phrase has become a set expression in Norwegian.

## 4.1 What Is the Network Commitment?

As mentioned in Section 1.1, Cognitive Grammar's network commitment boils down to the idea that all linguistic categories constitute networks of subcategories that are connected through categorizing relationships, a position that is shared by most, if not all varieties of cognitive linguistics (Diessel 2019). Figure 8 provides a representation of a Cognitive Grammar network in its simplest form. The network consists of a prototypical subcategory with some content, here represented as XY and a non-prototypical subcategory XZ. The two subcategories are connected through a general schema in the top portion of the diagram, which contains the information shared by both subcategories, viz. X.

Categorizing relationships are represented as arrows and are of two types. The solid arrows represent instantiation relations, that is, relations between fully compatible schemas of different degrees of specificity (Langacker 1987: 371). The arrows point towards the more specific schemas that are subtypes of the more general schema. In Figure 8, both XY and XZ are subtypes of X in the same way as sparrows and ostriches are subtypes of the general schema for birds.

Dashed arrows represent the categorizing relationships that Langacker (1987: 371) refers to as 'extensions'. Extension relationships hold between partly compatible schemas. In Figure 8, the subcategories XY and XZ are similar, but neither is a subtype of the other, much in the same way as sparrows and ostriches are somewhat similar, although neither is a subtype of the other. The extension relation in Figure 8 takes the prototype as its starting point, here XY. The prototype may be defined as the subcategory that is most representative of the category as a whole (Lewandowska-Tomaszczyk 2007). For instance, sparrows may be considered more representative for the category of birds as a whole than ostriches. After all, ostriches are atypical birds since they do not fly.

In Figure 8, the prototype is represented as a box with thicker lines, which indicates a high degree of entrenchment. Langacker describes entrenchment as follows:

> Linguistic structures are [...] conceived as falling along a continuous scale of entrenchment in cognitive organization. Every use of a structure has a positive impact on its degree of entrenchment, whereas extended periods of disuse have a negative impact. With repeated use, a novel structure becomes progressively entrenched, to the point of becoming a unit.
>
> (Langacker 1987: 59)

What this means is that schemas become more entrenched in the mental grammar of speakers through repetition. This implies that – other things being equal – elements of high frequency are more entrenched than elements of lower

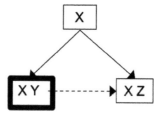

**Figure 8** A simple category network in Cognitive Grammar

frequency. However, the exact relationship between frequency and entrenchment is far from simple and has been the subject of considerable discussion in
cognitive linguistics (Schmid 2014, 2015, 2017, 2020 and Divjak 2019).

In generative linguistics, language has traditionally been conceptualized as
consisting of a lexicon (an unstructured list of words) and a syntax (a set of rules
generating sentences based on the input from the lexicon). The network commitment of Cognitive Grammar implies a different approach. Instead of a model
consisting of separate modules, Cognitive Grammar assumes that all of language can be conceptualized as one large category network. Langacker (1987,
1991a, 2008, 2013) refers to the nodes of the network as 'schemas', but in recent
years it has become increasingly common to use the term 'construction' about
pairings of meaning and form (Goldberg 1995, 2006). Accordingly, the entire
category network of a language can be termed a 'constructicon' (Lyngfelt et al.
2018). A number of constructicons (models of mental grammars) for different
languages are being built, including one for Russian (Janda et al. 2018).

A category network may represent the state of a language at some point in
time, but the network commitment also has implications for the analysis of
language change. As we will see in the following section, semelfactive verbs in
Russian provide an example of the emergence and development of a category
network over time.

## 4.2 An Expanding Network: Semelfactive Verbs

### 4.2.1 Prototypical Semelfactives: Four Features

Recall from Section 3.2 that semelfactive verbs with the *-nu* suffix typically
denote a punctual event, or as suggested by Zaliznjak and Šmelev (2000: 118),
'one quantum of the activity described by the base verb'. Thus, the semelfactive
verb *maxnut'* 'wave once', denotes one single event ('quantum') of waving, as
opposed to its base verb *maxat'* 'wave' which may describe a series of waving
events. In Section 3.2, we explored the relationship between the semelfactive
*-nu* suffix and the homophonous inchoative suffix. In what follows, we will

consider the emergence and gradual development of the semelfactive category over time. It will be shown that we are dealing with an expanding category network that illustrates how the network commitment provides the historical linguist with a valuable analytical tool.

While Zaliznjak and Šmelev's (2000) definition is helpful as far as it goes, a more detailed description involving four features is explored in Nesset (2013: 125–9). The first feature is 'uniformity'. In most cases, semelfactive verbs are related to base verbs denoting activities that consist of uniform subevents. Thus, *maxat'* describes a series of waving events that for all practical purposes are identical. Admittedly, semelfactives are occasionally formed from activity verbs that do not involve uniform subevents. A case in point is *rabotnut'* 'do one lick of work', which is formed from the activity verb *rabotat'* 'work'. Clearly, this verb may involve very different tasks, such as write an academic paper, teach a class, participate in an administrative meeting, and other tasks familiar to most university employees. However, verbs like *rabotnut'* are not prototypical semelfactive verbs, as illustrated by the fact that *rabotnut'* is attested only three times in the Russian National Corpus, which contains more than 330 million words.[14]

The second feature describing prototypical semelfactives is 'instantaneous-ness', meaning that the relevant verbs are construed as having minimal duration. As pointed out in Nesset (2013: 126), verbs like *maxnut'* felicitously combine with punctual adverbials such as *vdrug* 'suddenly' and *vnezapno* 'suddenly', thus indicating that the events are conceptualized as instantaneous. While instantaneousness characterizes *prototypical* semelfactive verbs, there are exceptions, such as Isačenko's (1974: 398) famous example *kutnut'* 'to go on a binge', which may involve partying for some time.

Prototypical semelfactives furthermore are non-resultative; as opposed to most perfective verbs in Russian, semelfactive verbs do not culminate in a change of state (Nesset 2013: 126). A non-semelfactive perfective such as *napisat'* 'write (perfective)' denotes the transition from a state where something is not written to a state where a written document has come into existence. Semelfactives like *maxnut'* 'wave once', on the other hand, do not involve such a change of state. When you have performed one act of waving, your hand goes back to the initial position so that you are ready to carry out a new waving act. Once again, exceptions are possible, as shown by examples such as *prygnut' čerez zabor* 'jump over a fence' where the jumper ends up on the other side of the fence. However, examples of this type do not represent the prototypical usage of semelfactive verbs (Nesset 2013: 126).

---

[14] The Russian National Corpus (www.ruscorpora.ru) was consulted on August 9, 2021.

The fourth feature characteristic of prototypical semelfactives is that they tend to denote single occurrences. Typically, *maxnut'* involves one single waving act. Nevertheless, contexts with certain quantifiers may force readings of repeated events, as in the following example, where the person in question waves more than once with a machete:

(25)     Maxnu-v     par-u      raz          tesak-om,     on       skaza-l [. . .].
         Wave-       couple-    time[GEN.    machete-      he       say-PST.M
         GERUND      ACC.SG     PL]          INS.SG        [NOM]
         'After having waved with the machete a couple of times, he said [. . .]'
         (Ivanov 1990–1)

With the four features in mind – uniformity, instantaneousness, non-resultativity, and single occurrence – we will now investigate how far back in the history of the Slavic languages we can trace prototypical semelfactive verbs.

### 4.2.2 The Emergence of Semelfactives: Evidence from Old Church Slavonic

Since semelfactive verbs are attested in the modern languages of all three branches of the Slavic languages (South, East, and West), we would expect the semelfactive category to be inherited from Common Slavic. We do not have any written records from (early) Common Slavic, but the Old Church Slavonic text corpus (OCS, see text box) from the tenth to eleventh centuries give some indications of the situation in Late Common Slavic, the final stage of the period when the entire Slavic area could be considered one single language. As we will see, the OCS texts contain examples suggesting that the semelfactive category existed, at least in an embryonic version.

OLD CHURCH SLAVONIC (OCS)

The oldest texts in Slavic are referred to as 'Old Church Slavonic', which may be defined as non-East Slavic texts from before 1100 AD. This text canon derives from the work of two brothers, Constantine (who later took the name Cyril when he became a monk) and Methodius. In the fall of 863 AD, they came to Moravia, invited by Duke Rostislav, who had asked the Byzantine emperor to send missionaries who would teach the Gospel in Slavic instead of in Latin. Although the Moravian mission was not particularly successful, it represents a watershed in the history of the Slavic peoples, because Constantine and Methodius translated key texts from the New Testament using a new alphabet they had devised for the purpose. Therefore, the Moravian mission was the beginning of literacy in Slavic. Today, Russian uses the Cyrillic alphabet, which is named after Cyril. However, this is most likely *not* the alphabet that Cyril and his brother invented, since the oldest manuscripts are in the so-called Glagolitic alphabet. The OCS text canon contains a number of manuscripts in both alphabets, the oldest of which are from the tenth century. Read more about Old Church Slavic and the two alphabets in Nesset (2015: 33–6).

In Nesset (2012 and 2013), it is shown that OCS had seventy-eight attested verbs with the suffix -*nǫ*, the cognate of -*nu* in present-day Russian. However, the majority are either imperfective verbs (inchoatives/gradatives) or their prefixed perfective partner verbs, which are not directly relevant for present purposes, since in these verbs the -*nǫ* suffix does not signal semelfactivity and the prototypical semelfactives in present-day Russian are perfective verbs without a prefix. Of such verbs, we have fourteen in OCS, listed in Table 9. Are any of these verbs prototypical semelfactive verbs? In Nesset (2013: 131–2), two sets of verbs are singled out as early examples of semelfactives. In the following we will explore one of these sets, viz. the 'mouth-based' verbs *dunǫti* 'blow', *plinǫti* 'spit', *plunǫti* 'spit', and *zinǫti* 'yawn'.[15]

As pointed out in Nesset (2013: 132), the lexical meanings of verbs of spitting, blowing, and yawning make them excellent candidates for semelfactive verbs, since they conform to the four criteria discussed in Section 4.2.1. They are all activities that involve uniform subevents ('quants'), and they can easily be conceptualized as instantaneous.[16] In addition, they are not resultative, in the sense that they do not lead to a change of state. Rather, when one spitting 'quant' is carried out, the mouth goes back to its initial state, and is ready to carry out another spitting event. In other words, spitting resembles waving, inasmuch as the body goes back to the initial state when one 'quant' has been performed. With regard to the fourth feature, single occurrence, the lexical meaning of the verbs is not sufficient to determine whether the verbs in question are used about single or repeated events. However, the analysis in Nesset (2013: 132–7) shows that the relevant verbs tended to be used about single events.

Let us consider one typical text example, illustrating how the use of *plinǫti* conforms to the four features of prototypical semelfactive verbs:

---

[15] I represent examples from Old Church Slavic and Old East Slavic in transliterated orthography. Notice that the relevant examples are from before the jer shift described in Section 2.2. As is customary in Slavic linguistics, the jers are represented as ъ (phonemic /ŭ/) and ь (phonemic /ĭ/) in the examples.

[16] It should be pointed out that most verbs are polysemous, and that not all uses conform to all criteria. Consider *dut'* 'blow'. Blowing air into a balloon may be described as an activity that consists of uniform subevents ('quants'), while in the collocation *duet veter* 'a wind is blowing' it is less clear that we are dealing with uniform subevents.

**Table 9** All unprefixed perfective OCS verbs with the -nǫ suffix, adapted from Nesset 2013: 131

| Verb | Gloss | Number of attestations: |
|---|---|---|
| *drъznǫti* | 'take courage, be bold' | 31 |
| *goneznǫti* | 'avoid' | 10 |
| *minǫti* | 'pass by' | 10 |
| *dvignǫti* | 'move' | 26 |
| *mrъknǫti* | 'get dark' | 8 |
| *vyknǫti* | 'learn, get used to' | 5 |
| *kanǫti* | 'drip' | 1 |
| *dunǫti* | 'blow' | 4 |
| *plinǫti/pljunǫti* | 'spit' | 14 |
| *zinǫti* | 'yawn' | 2 |
| *kosnǫti* | 'touch' | 43 |
| *rinǫti* | 'push' | 1 |
| *tlъknǫti* | 'knock' | 8 |
| *tъknǫti* | 'strike, pierce, wound' | 2 |
| Total number of attestations | | 165 |

(26) Si      rek-ъ         **plinǫ**        na       zeml-jǫ          i
     this    say-PTCP.M.SG  spit            on       ground-ACC.SG    and
                           [AORIST.3SG]

     sъtvori  breni-e       otъ      plinoveni-ě       i        pomaza
     create   mud-ACC.SG    from     saliva-GEN.SG     and      smear
     [AORIST.3SG]                                               [AORIST.3SG]

     emu      oč-i          brъnь-emь.
     he[DAT]  eye-ACC.DU    mud-INS.SG

'Having said this, he **spat** on the ground, made some mud with the saliva, and put it on the man's eyes.' (John 9:6, Codex Marianus, PROIEL corpus)[17]

We are here dealing with a single occurrence of a uniform and instantaneous spitting event that is part of a sequence of completed single events. The event is furthermore not resultative in the relevant sense; although the spitting is carried out in order to achieve a goal, the focus is not on what happens to the ground

---

[17] The PROIEL corpus is available at www.hf.uio.no/ifikk/english/research/projects/proiel/.

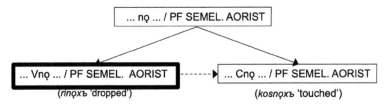

**Figure 9** Semelfactive aorists in OCS (SEMEL. = semelfactive, PF = perfective)

after Jesus spits on it, but rather what happens to the blind man who is cured by Jesus (Nesset 2013: 133–4).

Two further observations can be made about the use of verbs like *plinǫti* in OCS. First, most examples concern the aorist, a past tense form that is typically used about single events in the past. Second, in the relevant verbs the -*nǫ* suffix is most often preceded by a vowel as in *plinǫti*, although verbs with a consonant before the suffix are also attested (e.g., *kosnǫti* 'touch', see, e.g., Stang 1942: 55, Diels 1963: 258, and Gorbachov 2007: 41 for discussion).

In the context of Cognitive Grammar, we may postulate the category structure in Figure 9 for the semelfactive category in OCS. The schema in the lower left portion of the figure represents the prototype, viz. perfective aorists with a vowel preceding the -*nǫ* suffix. Thicker lines are used to represent the prototype. An extension relation represented as a dashed arrow leads from the prototype to the less numerous type with a consonant before the suffix. The upper portion of the figure contains a general schema that does not specify the sound before the suffix. This general schema is connected to the lower-level schemas by means of solid arrows, representing instantiation relations.

The category depicted in the figure suggests that there existed an association between the -*nǫ* suffix and semelfactive meaning but does not say anything about the strength of this association. This issue can be addressed in at least two different ways. First, we can consider the relationship between perfective verbs with -*nǫ* and perfective verbs without this suffix. Is there a division of labour, whereby the -*nǫ* verbs are exclusively used in the semelfactive meaning, whereas other perfective verbs fulfil other functions? Given the limited number of attestations in the OCS text corpus, it is impossible to give a definitive answer to this question. However, examples of the following type, discussed at length in Nesset (2013: 134), suggest that such a division of labour may have been emerging:

(27)  Тъгда  **zaplьva-ša**     lic-e         ego   i      pakost-i        emu
      then    spit-AORIST.3PL  face-ACC.SG  his  and  damage-ACC.PL  he[DAT]
      děa-šę.
      do-AORIST.3PL
      'Then they **spat** in his face and struck him with their fists.' (Matthew 26:67)

Here, a perfective verb without the -*nǫ* suffix is used in what is arguably a resultative context. The soldiers spat Jesus in his face, which humiliated him. The humiliation was a direct consequence of the spitting, and the spitting thus produces a change of state from not humiliated to humiliated. This is different from the example with the -*nǫ* suffix in (26), where the spitting itself had no direct effect on the blind man. Admittedly, the difference between the two examples is subtle, but it is nevertheless suggestive of an emerging division of labour between perfective verbs with and without the -*nǫ* suffix. An additional reason for not using a semelfactive verb in (27) is the fact that the spitting was carried out by several soldiers, so in a sense we are dealing with a number of spitting events, rather than one single event.

A second way of addressing the strength of the association between the -*nǫ* suffix and semelfactive semantics is in terms of cue validity, that is, the conditional probability that an item belongs to a particular category given a particular feature ('cue', see Bates and MacWhinney 1987, and Goldberg 2006: 105 for discussion). In our case, the relevant cue is -*nǫ*, and the question is to what extent it is possible to predict that a verb has semelfactive meaning on the basis of the -*nǫ* suffix. As shown in Nesset (2013: 143), the cue validity is between 0.4 and 0.6, depending on whether one compares with all unprefixed perfective -*nǫ* verbs or limits oneself to a smaller set of verbs with certain morphophonological properties characteristic of semelfactive verbs. Cue validity between 0.4 and 0.6 indicates that the semelfactive meaning can be predicted with 40 per cent to 60 per cent accuracy. These are not very high values, but they are comparable to the cue validities discussed by Goldberg (2006: 107) for constructions in modern English.

Taken together, the available evidence from OCS suggests that the semelfactive category was emerging and had reached an embryonic state towards the end of the Common Slavic period. In the next sections, we will follow the expansion of the semelfactive category from Old East Slavic to present-day Russian.

### 4.2.3 Expansion to New Types of Verbs: Old and Middle Russian

Russian has excellent historical dictionaries that make it possible to study the gradual development of the semelfactive category through the Old and Middle Russian periods (eleventh to seventeenth centuries). The data to be explored in the following are excerpted from Sreznevskij (1893–1906) and *Slovar' russkogo jazyka XI-XVII vv.* (1975–), as discussed in detail in Nesset (2013). A total of eighty-eight unprefixed perfective verbs with the -*nu* suffix are attested in the dictionaries. Of these verbs, forty-eight can be classified as semelfactives. This yields a cue validity of 0.6, which is comparable to the cue validities attested in the OCS data discussed in the previous section. Clearly, the semelfactive category became consolidated in Old and Middle Russian.

Detailed analysis of the relevant verbs corroborates the conclusion from the preceding section that bodily acts formed the basis for the semelfactive category. Of the forty-eight semelfactive verbs under scrutiny, thirty-two can be classified as bodily acts, such as *pljunuti* 'spit' and *maxnuti* 'wave' (Nesset 2013: 146–7). Such verbs are attested from the earliest Old East Slavic sources, dating back to the eleventh century. The following example from the *Primary Chronicle* shows that in Old East Slavic *pljunuti* was used in the same way as its cognate in OCS:

(28)  Si      slyša-v-ъ,        Volodimir-ъ        **pljunu**          na  zeml-ju,
      this    hear-PTCP-M.SG    Volodimir-NOM.SG   spit[AORIST.3SG]    on  ground-ACC.SG
      rek-ъ:' 'Nečist-o         estь               děl-o'
      say-PTCP.M.SG  dirty-NOM.SG.N  be[PRS.3SG]   thing-NOM.SG
      'When he heard this, Vladimir **spat** on the ground and said: "This is dirty business."' (*Primary Chronicle*)[18]

In the same way as in example (26) in Section 4.2.2, this example describes a single occurrence of a uniform and instantaneous spitting event that is part of sequence of completed single events. The event is not resultative, in the sense that the spitting does not lead to a change of state, so we are dealing with a prototypical semelfactive situation.

What is of particular interest in the Old East Slavic data, is that we see evidence that the semelfactive category was spreading to other types of verbs than bodily acts. Thirteen verbs are 'auditory verbs', that is, verbs where an animal or human subject produces a sound (Nesset 2013: 149–50). Examples include *brexnuti* 'yelp, bark once', *kriknuti* 'scream once', and *svistnuti* 'whistle once'. Consider the following example from the *Igor Tale*, the medieval poem that forms the basis for Borodin's famous opera *Prince Igor*:

(29)  Komon-ь      vъ    polunoč-i       Ovlur-ъ            **svisnu**
      horse-NOM.SG in    midnight-LOC.SG Ovlur-NOM.SG       whistle[AORIST.3SG]
      za           rěk-oju [...].
      beyond       river-INS.SG
      'Bringing a horse at midnight, Ovlur **whistled** beyond the river [...]' (Igor Tale)

---

[18]  The example is cited from http://lib.pushkinskijdom.ru/Default.aspx?tabid=4869.

Although we cannot know for sure exactly what kind of sound Ovlur, the captive Igor's helper, produced, it stands to reason that he would make one instantaneous high-pitched sound of minimal duration, so as to prevent the guards who were watching over Igor from becoming suspicious. If so, we are dealing with a prototypical semelfactive usage. The *Igor Tale* describes historical events that took place in 1185 AD, and on the reasonable assumption that the poem was created shortly after these events, example (29) testifies to the existence of auditory semelfactive verbs at the end of the twelfth century. Read more about the *Igor Tale* in the text box.

THE AUTHENTICITY OF THE *IGOR TALE*

The authenticity of the *Igor Tale* has been questioned by a number of scholars, since the only existing medieval copy was lost in a fire in the early nineteenth century. However, Russian linguist Andrej Zaliznjak (2008b) has conclusively demonstrated its authenticity. The text displays consistent use of many linguistic features such as clitics that were not well understood by linguists two hundred years ago. Only a linguistic genius could have forged such a text. In addition, this anonymous forger would have mastered Old East Slavic without access to adequate grammars or dictionaries, and then been able to write a literary masterpiece in this language. In addition, an anonymous forger would have had to keep his tremendous knowledge completely secret to his contemporaries. Zaliznjak laconically describes the formidable task of an anonymous forger as follows: 'Hitting an ace of hearts blindfolded using a pistol slung facing backwards over your shoulder is a mere trifle compared to such a task' (Zaliznjak 2008b: 96).

While bodily acts and auditory verbs constitute the majority of attested semelfactive verbs in Old and Middle Russian, the dataset explored in Nesset (2013) also contains two optical verbs, viz. *blesnuti* and *melьkanuti,* which both mean 'flash'. An early attestation concerns the description of year 1389 in one of the medieval chronicles:

(30)  **Blesnu-ša**        oruži-a,        aki    molni-a          vъ    den-ь
      flash-AORIST.3PL  weapon-NOM.PL  like  lightning-NOM.SG  in    day-ACC.SG
      **dožd-ja** . . .
      rain-GEN.SG
      'Their weapons **flashed** like the lightning on a rainy day [. . .] ' (*Polnoe sobranie russkix letopisej* vol. 11, page 111)

Since the flashing of the weapons are compared to the lightning, we are likely dealing with an instantaneous flash (i.e., a prototypical usage of a semelfactive verb). This suggests that optical semelfactive verbs were in use in the fourteenth to fifteenth centuries; while the relevant chronicle is preserved in manuscripts from the sixteenth century (Kloss 1980: 4), it is likely that the language of the chronicle reflects usage closer to the historical events in 1389.

The data from Old and Middle Russian contain one verb of motion: *nyrnuti* 'dash off, disappear suddenly':[19]

(31)  Makar-ъ       Antioxijsk-ij       zaběža-l-ъ   vъ  Gruz-i,      jako
      Makar-NOM.SG  of_Antiox-NOM.SG    flee-PST-M.SG  in  Gruz-ACC.PL  like
      pes-ъ    otъ    volk-a        v  podvorotn-ju   **nyrnu-l-ъ**.
      dog-NOM.SG  from  wolf-GEN.SG   in  under_gate-ACC.SG  dive-PST-M.SG
      'M. A. fled to G. like a dog that escaped from a wolf by **dashing** under a
      gate.' (Avvakum 1677 cited after *Slovar' russkogo jazyka XI-XVII vv.* 1975–)

Since the example describes the sudden movement of a dog that manages to escape from a wolf, we seem to be dealing with a semelfactive verb that describes one single occurrence of a uniform and instantaneous event. The example is from 1677, thus testifying to the existence of semelfactive verbs of motion in the seventeenth century. In the same way as prototypical semelfactives, *nyrnuti* may be used in a non-resultative way, for instance when a duck goes under water, then comes back to the surface to prepare for its next dive. However, in (31) the verb involves a change of state, insofar as the subject manages to escape from danger.

From the perspective of Cognitive Grammar, we can portray the development as the gradual growth of a category network. The development starts with the most numerous and oldest subcategory, viz. bodily acts, which we may consider the prototype. The first addition is the subcategory of auditory verbs, which we may connect to the prototype through an extension relation represented as a dashed arrow in Figure 10. Later additions are the smaller subcategories of optical verbs and verbs of motion. A double-headed arrow connects auditory and optical verbs since these subcategories are closely related insofar as both involve sensory impressions.

---

[19] It should be pointed out that *nyrnuti* is not a prototypical motion verb (unlike, say, the verbs for 'walk', 'run', etc.). As an anonymous reviewer points out, we cannot exclude the possibility that semelfactive motion verbs have been with us since Late Common Slavic. A possible candidate of an early semelfactive verb of motion is *minǫti* 'pass by', mentioned in Table 9. However, a detailed discussion of the meaning and use of this verb is beyond the scope of the present study.

The extension relations are metonymic, that is, contiguity relations of the PART–WHOLE and CAUSE–EFFECT types. Bodily acts involve the movement of a body part (e.g., the hand), while verbs of motion imply that the whole body moves. This metonymic extension relation is therefore of the PART–WHOLE type. Auditory verbs are related to bodily acts through a CAUSE–EFFECT metonymy, since the production of sound (e.g., when you whistle) is the result of the movement of a body part. In a similar fashion, optical verbs involve a body part, namely the eyes, but the focus is not on the activity of the eyes per se, but rather on the optical impressions connected to the eye activity. It is likely that the expansion of the category network involved the emergence of new general schemas that would connect the subcategories through instantiation relations. However, in order to create a reader-friendly diagram, such general schemas are not included.

Each subcategory in Figure 10 includes information about the meaning of the relevant verbs, their earliest attestations and the number of attested verbs. The thickness of the lines indicates the relative size of the subcategories (i.e., the number of attested verbs for each subcategory).

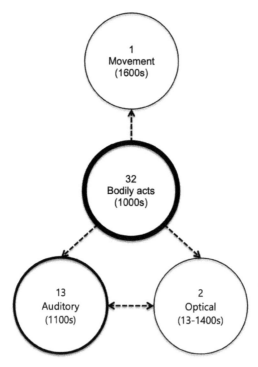

**Figure 10** The diachronic development of the semelfactive category network in Old and Middle Russian, adapted from Nesset 2013: 155. Numbers in parentheses represent century of innovation.

### 4.2.4 Further Expansion: Contemporary Standard Russian

Kuznetsova and Makarova (2012) conducted an empirical study of semelfactives in Contemporary Standard Russian. Their data indicate that the expansion of the semelfactive category to new types of verbs that took place in Old and Middle Russian continues in present-day Russian.

Kuznetsova and Makarova's data indicate the emergence of a subcategory of behavioural verbs (i.e., verbs denoting instantaneous episodes of certain behaviours). If we limit ourselves to well-established, conventionalized verbs with more than fifty attestations in the Russian National Corpus, the following verbs are represented in Kuznetsova and Makarova's data: *gul'nut'* 'make merry', *psixanut'* 'freak out', *ljapnut'* 'blurt out', *risknut'* 'take a risk', *kozyrnut'* 'play a trump', *šuganut'* 'scare off'. Here is a representative example from an internet forum:

(32)  Mož-et        za       semejn-ym       obed-om       **psixanu-t'**,
      may-3SG       behind   family-INS.SG.M  lunch-INS.SG  freak_out-INF

      vskoči-t',    zaplaka-t'  i                ubeža-t'.
      leap_up-INF   cry-INF     and              run_away-INF
      'At a family lunch, she may **freak out**, leap up, begin to cry and run away.'
      (*Ženščina + mužčina: Brak*, 2004)

The example describes a sudden emotional outburst, and thus represents a prototypical usage of a semelfactive verb.

The subcategory of auditory verbs also presents evidence of further expansion of the semelfactive category. While in Old and Middle Russian the auditory verbs predominantly involved sounds produced through the mouth (e.g., *svistnut'* 'whistle'), Kuznetsova and Makarova's data from Contemporary Standard Russian involve a number of other verbs denoting sounds, such as *zvjaknut'* 'jingle, tinkle once' and *skripnut'* 'squeak once'. The following example illustrates the prototypical usage of semelfactive verbs involving single occurrences of uniform, instantaneous and non-resultative events:

(33)  Pripodnja-l-sja   i        se-l,            stara-ja-s'          ne
      Get_up-PST.M.     and      sit-PST.M.SG     try-GERUND-REFL      not
      SG-REFL

      dyša-t'           i        ne               dviga-t'-sja,        čtob          ne
      breathe-INF       and      not              move-INF-REFL        in_order_to   not

      **skripnu-l**     divan.
      squeak-PST.M.SG   sofa[NOM.SG]
      'He got up and sat, trying not to breathe and move, so that the sofa would not **squeak**.' (Azol'skij 1997)

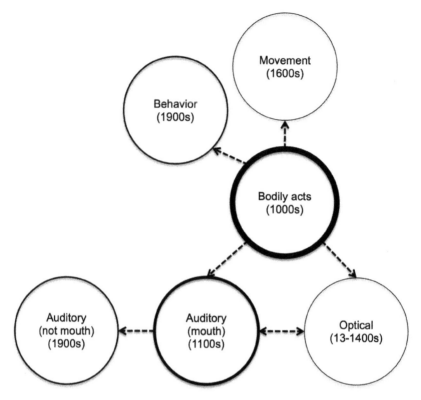

**Figure 11** The development of the semelfactive category in Modern Russian

If we include the behavioural semelfactives and divide the auditory verbs into two groups, 'mouth-based' and 'not mouth-based', we arrive at the category network in Figure 11. The behavioural verbs are treated as an extension from the prototype, since behaviours such as freaking out involve bodily reactions, although the focus is on the meaning of these reactions in a social setting, rather than the body itself. The not mouth-based auditory verbs are analysed as an extension from the mouth-based auditory verbs. The thickness of the lines in the figure offers an approximate size of each subcategory (measured as the number of attested examples in Kuznetsova and Makarova's (2012) dataset.

## 4.3 Summing Up the Network Commitment in Diachronic Linguistics

This detailed analysis of the history of the semelfactive verbs in Russian demonstrates that the network commitment provides Cognitive Grammar with a powerful tool for the analysis of language change. Two points are of particular importance. First, we have seen that category networks help us understand and analyse the emergence of grammatical categories. In Late Common Slavic, the association between the *-nǫ* suffix and semelfactive can be analysed in terms of a network consisting of a prototype (V-final roots) and a non-prototypical subcategory (C-final roots), as well as a more general schema connecting the two subcategories by means of instantiation relations. This is indeed an example of Langacker's (1987: 74) classic configuration in Figure 8 in Section 4.1.

The second important point illustrated by our analysis of the Russian semelfactive pertains to the gradual development of grammatical categories over time. Once the semelfactive category had established itself in Late Common Slavic, it started to expand to metonymically related verbs, a development that is still going on in present-day Russian. This development can be analysed as the addition of new subcategories to the category network through extension relations from the prototypical subcategory. The extension relations we have investigated are metonymic in nature, but Cognitive Grammar also acknowledges other mechanisms, such as metaphor, as the basis for the expansion of a category network.

## 5 The Usage-Based Commitment

### 5.1 What Is the Usage-Based Commitment?

As pointed out in Section 1.1, the usage-based commitment of Cognitive Grammar is the idea that grammar emerges through usage. According to Cognitive Grammar, a grammar is not part of an innate language faculty that generates correct sentences based on input from a lexicon. Instead, as shown in Section 4.1, a grammar is conceptualized as a network of generalizations that emerge from language use in a bottom-up fashion. In view of this, it is not surprising that Langacker sometimes refers to his framework as the 'usage-based model' (Langacker 1991b: 261–88, and 1999: 91–145), a term also used by Bybee (2001). For recent discussions of the usage-based commitment, see Diessel (2019) and Divjak (2019).

The usage-based approach explains why Cognitive Grammar goes hand in hand with corpus linguistics. Electronic corpora, such as the Russian National Corpus, provide large amounts of authentic linguistic examples representing concrete usage events. Corpus data therefore form an excellent basis for the study of generalizations emerging from language use. We have explored corpus data in Sections 2 and 3. In what follows, we will be concerned with two implications of a usage-based approach to diachronic linguistics. In Section 5.2, we will see that the usage-based commitment facilitates an insightful analysis of multiple motivation in historical linguistics. Section 5.3 explores the importance of quantitative analysis for a usage-based approach to language change.

## 5.2 Multiple Motivation: The Cocktail Hypothesis and Case Marking of Objects

### 5.2.1 The Descriptive Problem

From everyday life we know that our behaviour may be motivated by a multiplicity of factors. How did you choose your profession? How did you end up living where you live? It is often futile to pinpoint one single reason behind each choice, because there are so many factors that are relevant. My idea is that language is similar. I propose that language change is frequently the result of multiple motivation, that is, that change is driven by a multiplicity of factors that interact in non-trivial ways. Metaphorically speaking, we may refer to this idea as the 'cocktail hypothesis', since a cocktail is a mixed drink, the taste of which depends on the interaction of its various ingredients (Nesset 2016b). The challenge facing us as linguists is to capture the interplay of factors. I argue that category networks based on data from authentic language use show us the way to meet this challenge. We will focus on an ongoing change in the case marking of grammatical objects in Russian, which provides a good illustration of multiple motivation and the cocktail hypothesis.

The descriptive problem posed by case marking is simple. While most Russian verbs combine with objects in the accusative case, some verbs govern other cases – the dative, instrumental, or genitive. However, some of the verbs that traditionally govern the genitive also combine with accusative objects. A good example is *bojat'sja* 'fear'. In (34) the object is the genitive form *papy* of *papa* 'dad', whereas (35) has the accusative form *papu* of the same word.

(34)  Mam-a,      ja       bo-ju-s'      pap-y
      mom-NOM.SG  I[NOM]   fear-1SG-REFL  dad-GEN.SG
      'Mom, I am afraid of daddy.' (Braude 1949)

(35)  Xote-l      skry-t',     boja-l-sja       pap-u
      want-PST.M  hide-INF     fear-PST.M-REFL  dad-ACC.SG
      'I wanted to hide it, I was afraid of daddy.' (Terexov 1997–2008)

Is this genitive–accusative rivalry the result of ongoing language change? And if so, what are the factors motivating this change? In the following sections, we explore a cocktail of factors including individuation, animacy, grammatical voice, directionality, and frequency.

## 5.2.2 Individuation and Animacy

A factor that is often said to be relevant for case marking of grammatical objects in Russian is animacy. The data from Nesset and Kuznetsova (2015a and 2015b) confirm this for the verbs under scrutiny. As shown in Table 10 and Figure 12, the accusative is mostly attested for animate objects, and in both the main and the newspaper corpora animate nouns are more likely to be in the accusative than are inanimate nouns. The differences are statistically significant with a moderate to large effect size.[20] The use of the accusative is more widespread in the newspaper subcorpus, which suggests that genre may be a relevant factor.

Experimental data from an online experiment with 409 participants confirm the relevance of animacy with the verb *bojat'sja* 'fear' (Nesset and Kuznetsova 2015b: 271). As shown in Table 11 and Figure 13, the accusative is more likely to be used for animate nouns, and once again the observed differences are statistically significant and display a moderate effect size.[21]

Does the observed rivalry between the accusative and genitive cases represent language change? Corpus data strongly suggest that the answer is 'yes'. Table 12 and Figure 14 show that for animate nouns the use of the accusative has increased over time.[22] Once again, the observed differences are statistically significant, and the effect size is moderate.[23]

In Nesset and Kuznetsova (2015a: 374–5), we discuss the well-known observation that animacy is related to the broader concept of individuation, defined as the conventional likelihood that something is viewed as an individual (Timberlake 1985). Since animates (at least humans) have free will and are able to express emotions and move around, they are more likely to be seen as individuals, and hence display a higher degree of individuation than inanimates. In view of this, the data presented in this section suggest that a high degree of individuation favours the use of the accusative with the verbs under scrutiny.

---

[20] For the main subcorpus, the aggregate numbers for all verbs were compared. Pearson's Chi-squared test with Yates' continuity correction (X-squared = 1605.698, df = 1) returned a p-value < 2.2e-16. Cramer's V-value equals 0.4 (a moderate to large effect size). A very similar situation is observed in the newspaper subcorpus. Pearson's Chi-squared test with Yates' continuity correction (X-squared = 946.1605, df = 1) gave a p-value < 2.2e-16. Cramer's V-value is 0.4.

[21] Pearson's Chi-squared test with Yates' continuity correction gave the following results: X-squared = 890.72, df = 1, p-value < 2.2e-16. Cramer's V-value = 0.33, which indicates a moderate effect size.

[22] Note that Rusakova (2013: 331) found a similar development for the use of the accusative with negated transitive verbs.

[23] Comparison of the first period (1825–49) and the last period (2000–) yields a statistically significant difference, insofar as Pearson's Chi-squared test with Yates' continuity correction (X-squared = 5.224, df = 1) returns a p-value = 0.02. Cramer's V-value is 0.3, which indicates a moderate effect size. The statistical test suggests that we are dealing with slow increase that becomes evident over a period of two hundred years.

**Table 10** The distribution of accusative and genitive objects in two parts of the Russian National Corpus. The table gives aggregate numbers for five verbs: *bojat'sja* 'fear', *dožidat'sja* 'wait for', *dostigat'* 'reach', *izbegat'* 'avoid', and *slušat'sja* 'obey'. The rightmost column gives the percentage of the accusative, while the two columns with # contain raw numbers for the two cases under scrutiny. The data are adapted from Nesset and Kuznetsova (2015a: 375–6).

|  |  | #Accusative | #Genitive | %Accusative |
|---|---|---|---|---|
| Main subcorpus | animate | 170 | 561 | 23 |
|  | inanimate | 38 | 8,600 | <1 |
| Newspaper | animate | 79 | 13 | 86 |
| subcorpus | inanimate | 334 | 5,877 | 5 |

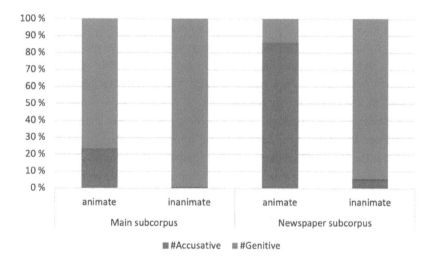

**Figure 12** The distribution of accusative and genitive objects in two parts of the Russian National Corpus, adapted from Nesset and Kuznetsova 2015a: 376

### 5.2.3 Grammatical Voice

In Nesset and Kuznetsova (2015a), we showed that there are considerable differences among the five verbs under scrutiny. *Slušat'sja* 'obey' is quite likely to combine with objects in the accusative, while *dostigat'* 'reach' and and *izbegat'* 'avoid' are less frequently attested with an accusative object. *Dožidat'sja* 'wait for' and *bojat'sja* 'fear' occupy intermediate positions. We can represent this as a hierarchy:

**Table 11** The distribution of accusative and genitive objects for the verb *bojat'sja* 'fear' in an online experiment, adapted from Nesset and Kuznetsova 2015b: 273

|           | #Accusative | #Genitive | %Accusative |
|-----------|-------------|-----------|-------------|
| Animate   | 1,726       | 2,336     | 42          |
| Inanimate | 518         | 3,527     | 13          |

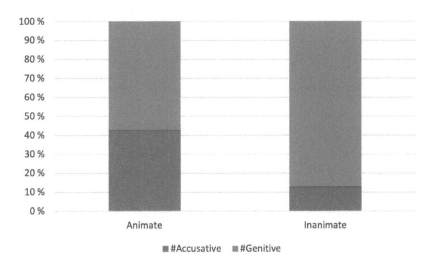

**Figure 13** The distribution of accusative and genitive objects for the verb *bojat'sja* 'fear' in an online experiment, adapted from Nesset and Kuznetsova 2015b: 273

(36)     Accusative-friendliness hierarchy:
         *slušat'sja* 'obey' > *dožidat'sja* 'wait for' > *bojat'sja* 'fear' > *dostigat'* 'reach', *izbegat'* 'avoid'

The question is now how we can explain the differences in the hierarchy. Why are some verbs more likely to combine with accusative objects than others? In this and the two following sections, we will explore three relevant factors.

The three verbs *bojat'sja* 'fear', *dožidat'sja* 'wait for', and *slušat'sja* 'obey' all contain the middle voice suffix *-sja*. Such verbs tend not to combine with accusative objects in modern Russian. This is no coincidence. Historically, *-sja* has developed from a pronominal clitic in the accusative. Since the object slot was originally filled by the accusative clitic, it was not possible for the verb to combine with another object in the accusative. The clitic gradually developed into a suffix in modern Russian (Nesset 1996, Nesset 1998: 264–72, Zaliznjak 2008a),

**Table 12** Changes in the use of the accusative for animate nouns of five verbs over time, adapted from Nesset and Kuznetsova 2015a: 381. The verbs included are *bojat'sja* 'fear', *doždat'sja* 'wait for', *dostigat'* 'reach, *izbegat'* 'avoid', and *slušat'sja* 'obey'.

| Time period | #Accusative | #Genitive | %Accusative |
|---|---|---|---|
| 1825–49 | 1 | 17 | 6 |
| 1850–74 | 7 | 24 | 23 |
| 1875–99 | 8 | 19 | 30 |
| 1900–24 | 8 | 26 | 24 |
| 1925–49 | 17 | 32 | 35 |
| 1950–74 | 19 | 20 | 49 |
| 1975–99 | 42 | 33 | 56 |
| 2000– | 37 | 26 | 59 |

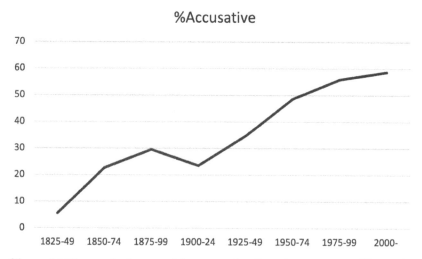

**Figure 14** Changes in the use of the accusative for animate nouns of five verbs over time, adapted from Nesset and Kuznetsova 2015a: 381

where it functions as a middle voice marker in the sense of Kemmer (1993). For instance, the middle voice verb *myt'sja* 'wash (oneself)' with *-sja* corresponds to the transitive verb *myt'* 'wash (someone/something)', which represents the active voice. However, *-sja* is polysemous and its meaning is not always transparent. In Nesset and Kuznetsova (2015a: 382), we propose that the more opaque the *-sja* suffix, the more likely the verb is to take an object in the accusative.

Detailed analysis of *bojat'sja*, *doždat'sja*, and *slušat'sja* suggests that this idea is on the right track, since for all three verbs *-sja* is rather opaque. While *myt'sja* 'wash' has a corresponding active verb (*myt'*), no such verb exists for *bojat'sja*. Therefore, it is not clear what grammatical meaning -*sja* contributes in *bojat'sja*. For *dožidat'sja* 'wait until' a corresponding verb *dožidat'* without -*sja* is attested in dialects (Filin 1972) but is generally not considered part of the standard language. With regard to *slušat'sja* 'obey', there is a corresponding verb without -*sja*, namely *slušat'* 'listen'. While 'obey' and 'listen' are related meanings, we are not dealing with any of the standard functions of the -*sja* suffix, so in the same way as in *bojat'sja* and *dožidat'sja, -sja* displays a relatively high degree of opacity in *slušat'sja*.

The upshot of this discussion is that grammatical voice seems to motivate the use of objects in the accusative, albeit in an indirect sense. The more opaque the semantic contribution of the middle voice marker -*sja*, the more likely is the verb to combine with an object in the accusative. While this observation does not provide a full explanation of the differences in the accusative-friendliness hierarchy, the three -*sja* verbs under scrutiny combine a high degree of opacity with a high degree of accusative-friendliness, as we would expect. It seems reasonable to argue that opacity of -*sja* promotes accusative-friendliness, and it is possible that some degree of opacity is a necessary condition for a verb with -*sja* to combine with objects in the accusative.

### 5.2.4 Directionality

A well-known insight about verbs governing the genitive case is that their meaning involves directionality towards or away from the object (Mathiassen 1996: 218 and Švedova 1980: 26). *Dostigat'* 'reach' involves motion towards a goal, while *izbegat'* 'avoid' implies a direction away from the object, and in this sense these verbs display a high degree of directionality. *Bojat'sja* is similar to *izbegat'*, since you avoid what you are afraid of. *Dožidat'sja* and *slušat'sja* are not related to directionality in a straightforward way, although both verbs involve paying attention to something or someone, which in an abstract sense presupposes directionality.

If we accept that directionality is a semantic property of verbs that govern the genitive, we expect the least directional verbs to be most likely to combine with objects in the accusative. In Nesset and Kuznetsova (2015a), we suggest that *dožidat'sja* and *slušat'sja* are least directional, and that this may be a partial explanation for why these verbs are more accusative-friendly than the other verbs under scrutiny. However, I hasten to add that there is no objective way to rank verbs according to directionality. Therefore, it is not possible to test the hypothesis about directionality and case usage in a rigorous way.

### 5.2.5 Frequency

In Section 3.2.1 on analogy, we saw that words tend to migrate from small classes to large classes. This is relevant for verbs governing the genitive and accusative cases. In Russian, accusative is the default option for grammatical objects; the vast majority of verbs that combine with an object mark that object in the accusative, including recent loans such as *guglit'* 'google' (as in *guglit'slovo* 'google a word'). The class of verbs that take genitive objects, on the other hand, is small and does not attract new members. This leads us to expect that verbs will migrate from the class that takes genitive objects to the class that combines with objects in the accusative – which is exactly what we observe.

Which individual verbs are most likely to change from genitive to accusative? It is well known in historical linguistics that low frequent lexical items are more likely to migrate from an unproductive to a productive class (Bybee 2007a). This leads us to expect that low-frequent genitive verbs will lead the migration process.

Table 13 ranks the verbs under scrutiny according to frequency based on data from the Russian National Corpus and Lyashevskaya and Sharoff (2009). Although the table does not provide a good match of the accusative-friendliness hierarchy, the fact that the least frequent verb, *slušat'sja* 'obey', shows the strongest tendency to combine with accusative objects offers some support to the idea that low frequency motivates the use of the accusative.

### 5.2.6 Usage-Based Generalizations: A Network Representation of Multiple Motivation

In the following, we will see how the interaction of the factors explored so far can be accommodated in a category network. This reinforces the conclusion made in Section 4 that the category network represents a valuable analytical tool in historical linguistics. However, in addition, the network I will present also supports the usage-based commitment. First, all the generalizations in question can be expressed as schemas that emerge from concrete usage events. For instance, the idea that individuation and animacy promote objects in the accusative can be analysed as a schema that has emerged and become entrenched as the use of accusative objects for animates increases. The more entrenched the schema becomes, the more likely it is to license the use of the accusative in new usage events.

A second point that supports the usage-based commitment concerns frequency. In Cognitive Grammar, schemas reflect differences in frequency directly. We have seen that frequency is relevant for the use of objects in the accusative, and

**Table 13** Five verbs ranked according to frequency. adapted from Nesset and
Kuznetsova 2015: 386

| Verb | RNC: occurrences | Frequency dictionary: ipm |
| --- | --- | --- |
| *bojat'sja* 'fear' | 3,468 | 266.5 |
| *dostigat'* 'reach' | 2,417 | 35.2 |
| *dožidat'sja* 'wait for' | 1,479 | 26.5 |
| *izbegat'* 'avoid' | 1,785 | 21.9 |
| *slušat'sja* 'obey' | 784 | 14.1 |

through schemas with different degrees of entrenchment we can capture this
generalization in a straightforward way in category networks.

Let us consider the network in Figure 15, which represents the multiple
motivation of accusative objects in terms of the factors discussed in the previous
sections.

Since this is a network in a usage-based model, its starting point is the
individual verbs in the bottom portion of the figure. Each verb is represented
as two schemas since all verbs combine with objects in two different cases. The
schemas for objects in the genitive (to the right) are instantiations of schema (d),
which captures the generalizations that a group of verbs with -*sja* and directional semantics take objects in the genitive. Schema (d) competes with the
more entrenched schema (b), whose box has thicker lines. Schema (b) accommodates the generalization that verbs in the active voice combine with objects in
the accusative – the default pattern for case marking of objects in Russian.
Schema (c) is a special case of this that represents the generalization that some
verbs with -*sja* combine with animate objects in the accusative. The specifica-
tion 'ACT' on the verb in schema (c) stands for active voice and expresses that
accusative objects are only possible when -*sja* is not a transparent marker of
middle voice. Schema (c) has three instantiations – the three verbs with accusative objects.

The arrows connecting schemas (c) and (d) with the individual verbs are in
different degrees of thickness. The thicker the line, the more closely is the verb
associated with the relevant schema. In this way, we capture the generalization
that the most frequent verb (*bojat'sja*, included in a thick box), is most likely to
take objects in the genitive, while *slušat'sja* (whose box has thin lines) is most
prone to combine with accusative objects.

Since Cognitive Grammar is a usage-based model, the network is constructed
in a bottom-up fashion. The schemas higher up in the figure emerge through
language use. The least important schema is schema (a) in the top portion of the

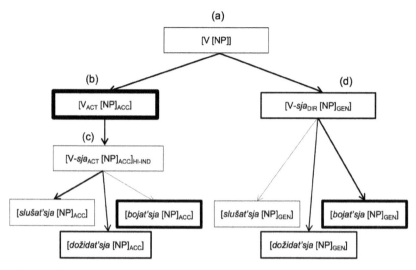

**Figure 15** Category network for accusative-genitive variation and change, adapted from Nesset and Kuznetsova 2015a: 388. ACC = accusative, ACT = active, DIR = directional, GEN = genitive, HI-IND = highly individuated (animate)

figure. While schema (a) brings the left and right portions of the network together through its instantiation relations, schema (a) merely says that verbs may combine with objects.

Although the category network in Figure 15 does not do justice to all facets of the rivalry between genitive and accusative objects in Russian, it suffices to show how a usage-based model accommodates frequency and other generalizations in category networks and thus captures the multiple motivation of case marking of objects in Russian.

The category network in Figure 15 can be interpreted as a synchronic analysis of present-day Russian, but at the same time it can be given a diachronic interpretation. Interpreted diachronically, schema (c) is an innovation that becomes more entrenched as the use of accusative objects with the verbs under scrutiny becomes more frequent. The diachronic interpretation is visualized in Video 5.

## 5.3 The Quantitative Turn: S-curves and Russian Numeral Constructions

In recent years, quantitative analysis has become part and parcel of cognitive linguistics, a development that Janda (2013) refers to as the 'quantitative turn'. The quantitative turn is a direct consequence of the usage-based commitment. If you are committed to analysing examples from authentic usage and you have access to an electronic corpus, you are likely to end up with a large dataset that requires statistical analysis. The quantitative turn may have hit historical linguistics relatively late, since diachronic corpora often are smaller and less developed than corpora of modern languages. However, the following case study illustrates the value of the usage-based commitment and quantitative analysis for the study of language change in Cognitive Grammar.

### 5.3.1 The S-curve Hypothesis

In Section 2.3, we explored the rivalry between the two constructions that correspond to *in the twenties* in English. Russian may use either the accusative or the locative case, but the use of the accusative has been on the increase over the past two centuries, as summarized in Figure 16. The curve is flat in the beginning, then shows a steep rise, before it flattens out towards the end. Curves of this shape are referred to as 'S-curves'.

S-curves have been considered crucial in language change, a generalization that has been referred to as 'Piotrowski's law' (Leopold 2005). Chambers (2002: 361) proposes that S-curves represent a 'kind of template for [language] change'. Blythe and Croft (2012: 280) claim that 'there are no clearly documented cases of change going toward completion that follows either a simple linear trajectory or an exponential curve'. S-curves have proved to be relevant for a number of diachronic phenomena, ranging from sound change (Labov 1994: 65–75) to syntactic change (Kroch 1989a, 1989b, 2003). The strongest possible hypothesis is that language change always takes the shape of an

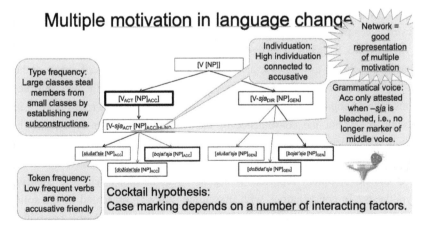

**Video 5** Changes in the case marking of objects – multiple motivation and the cocktail hypothesis (video available at www.cambridge.org/nesset-resources)

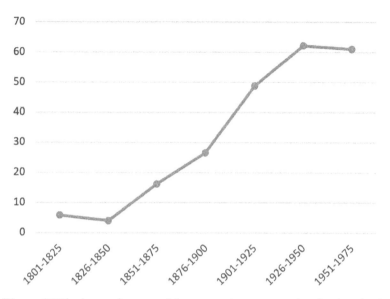

**Figure 16** The increasing use of the accusative construction for decades in
Russian (per cent based on the year of birth of the authors)

S-curve. We may refer to this as the 'S-curve hypothesis'. In what follows, we
will be concerned with a complex case regarding Russian numerals.

### 5.3.2 Russian Numerals and S-curves

Recall from Section 3.3 that the morphosyntax of Russian numerals has under-
gone a number of changes since medieval times, and that change is still in
progress. In the following, we will see that the ongoing development poses
challenges to the S-curve hypothesis, but that an analysis in terms of S-curves is
nevertheless possible.

In Section 3.3, we saw that Russian has two ways to express things like 'two new
apartments'. Either the adjective has the ending *-yx* as in *dve novyx kvartiry*, or the
ending *-ye* is used as in *dve novye kvartiry*. The rivalry between the two constructions reflects ongoing language change (Nesset 2020), as shown in Figure 7 in
Section 3.3.2. For the convenience of the reader, the diagram is repeated in
Figure 17, which displays the percentage of the *-yx* construction for different
time periods. As shown, the development depends on the gender of the noun.

Is the development reported in Figure 17 in harmony with the S-curve
hypothesis? In constructions with masculine nouns, represented as the solid
line in Figure 17, the answer seems to be 'yes'. The solid line has a flat
beginning, then rises steeply, before it flattens out towards the end – exactly
as predicted by the S-curve hypothesis.

The situation for constructions with neuter nouns represents a somewhat less clear case, as suggested by the dotted line in Figure 17. As predicted by the S-curve hypothesis, the relevant curve displays a steep rise before it flattens out towards the end. However, the beginning of the curve does not have the expected flat beginning. There may at least be three reasons for that (Nesset 2020: 533). First, we cannot exclude that the dataset underlying the study of the numerals is too small to bring out the precise shape of the curve. Second, it may be that we do not have reliable data far enough back in time. Maybe, if we had reliable data from before 1825, we would be able to draw a perfect S-curve? Third, one may point out that the curves in Figure 17 conflate three different constructions involving the numerals *dva* 'two', *tri* 'three', and *četyre* 'four'. It is entirely possible that different numerals show different developments over time. However, we do not have enough data available to draw reliable curves for different numerals (Nesset 2020: 533). All three scenarios reflect the same underlying problem, which is likely to be familiar to most, if not all historical linguists: scarcity of data (Berdičevskis and Eckhoff 2014).

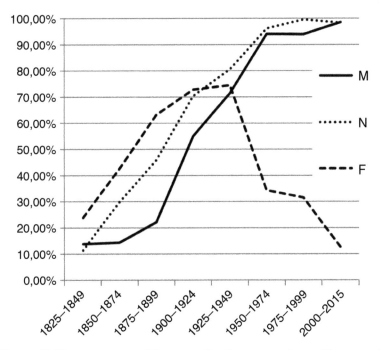

**Figure 17** The percentage of the -*yx* ending in constructions with a paucal numeral followed by an adjective and a masculine, feminine or neuter noun. For discussion, see also Section 3.3.2.

Constructions with feminine nouns, represented as a dashed line in Figure 17, pose more serious challenges to the S-curve hypothesis, since the dashed line describes a bell-shaped curve. Can this development be reconciled with the S-curve hypothesis? I argue that the answer is 'yes' – if one is willing to accept two manipulations, one trivial and one less so. Both manipulations are shown in Figure 18.

We start with the trivial manipulation. In Figure 17, evolution of the constructions with a feminine noun is measured as the percentage of *-yx* (which decreases from the middle of the twentieth century). In Figure 18, on the other hand, the change is represented as the percentage of *-ye*, which increases. Thus, in Figure 18 the blue lines represent the increase of *-yx* for masculine and neuter nouns, while the red line describes the increasing use of *-ye* in constructions with a feminine noun. While this manipulation does not involve any substantial change, it facilitates comparison with S-curves for constructions with nouns of all three genders.

The second and more controversial manipulation of the data in Figure 18 is that the oldest part of the evolution of the feminine construction has been removed. This is why. The feminines first followed a development that is roughly the same as the S-curves of the other genders, so the first part of the

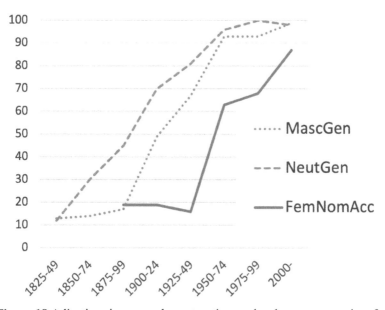

**Figure 18** Adjectives in numeral constructions – development over time for nouns of different genders. The curves in blue indicate the growing use of the genitive, while the red curve measures the increasing use of the nominative/ accusative. Adapted from Nesset 2020.

development of the feminines was therefore part of the general change that took place in all genders. Thus, it seems reasonable to say that the start of the development of the feminines is when they break off from the other genders. The red curve in Figure 18 captures this; it starts when the feminines diverge from the other genders and start a life on their own.

To what extent does the red curve in Figure 18 resemble an S-curve? It is flat in the beginning, and then displays a steep rise. Future linguists will be able to determine whether the curve will flatten out towards the end. As shown in Figure 18, the red curve does not contradict the S-curve hypothesis. However, the question is whether the manipulations underlying Figure 18 are legitimate. This is clearly a matter of interpretation, and it is not easy to establish clear and objective criteria.

The manipulations underlying Figure 18 illustrate how the usage-based commitment and the S-curve hypothesis raise important questions of interpretation that are of general interest to historical linguistics. However, at the same time, the proposed analysis shows that the usage-based commitment and the S-curve hypothesis also give rise to new hypotheses. Figure 18 brings out one aspect of the change under scrutiny that is not evident from Figure 17. The steep rise of the red curve in Figure 18 starts when the curves for the other genders have almost peaked and are about to flatten out. The question is whether this is a coincidence. I propose that it is not. I speculate that the use of *-yx* must have been established as a general rule before the feminines could monopolize the *-ye* ending (Nesset 2020: 535). Only when *-ye* was no longer widely used with masculine and neuter nouns, was this ending 'freed up' to be used with feminine nouns and could gradually turn into the rule for the feminine gender. We may state this idea in more general terms: Only when a general rule has been established, it is possible to deviate from it and create a new pattern. We may refer to this as the 'cascade hypothesis', since in Figure 18 we are dealing with a cascading effect, whereby a new S-curve starts when a previous S-curve is about to peak. Testing the cascade hypothesis is beyond the scope of the present study. What is at stake here, is to show that the usage-based commitment and the S-curve hypothesis leads to the creation of new hypotheses and therefore has the potential to further advance the study of language change in Cognitive Grammar.

## 5.4 Summing Up the Usage-Based Commitment in Diachronic Linguistics

Taken together, the case studies of case marking of objects and S-curves in numeral constructions has brought out two important facets of Cognitive

Grammar's usage-based commitment. First, we have seen that information from concrete usage events can be incorporated directly into category networks. In particular, the concept of entrenchment enables us to accommodate the relevance of frequency for language change in a straightforward way. The interaction of frequency and other usage-based factors in category networks makes Cognitive Grammar well equipped for the study of multiple motivation, situations where a 'cocktail' of factors interact in complex ways.

The second important point that emerges from the case studies is the fact that the usage-based commitment facilitates quantitative study of large sets of examples from language use. Quantitative analysis of this kind enables us to test important hypotheses about language change, such as the S-curve hypothesis that language change always follows an S-shaped curve. Furthermore, the usage-based commitment also leads to the advancement of new hypotheses, for example, the cascade hypothesis that a general rule needs to be established before it is possible to deviate from it and create a new pattern. In this way, both case studies testify to the fruitfulness of Cognitive Grammar's usage-based commitment for the study of language change.

## 6 Conclusion: Language Change in Cognitive Grammar

The present study has explored the intersection of three subfields of the language sciences: cognitive linguistics, historical linguistics, and Russian linguistics. The starting point has been four commitments that are cornerstones of Cognitive Grammar, but also shared by other varieties of cognitive linguistics. I refer to the idea that language is shaped by domain-general cognitive processes as the 'cognitive commitment', while the semiotic commitment is the analysis of language in terms of bipolar representations that connect form and meaning (and nothing else). I use the term 'network commitment' for the idea that these bipolar representations constitute one large network (the 'constructicon'). The idea that knowledge of language emerges from language use is labelled the 'usage-based commitment'.

Although the four commitments are well known, their implications for historical linguistics are understudied, especially when we go beyond studies of English. Through seven case studies I have shown that the four commitments offer fresh perspectives and new insights about language change, including foundational concepts such as sound change and analogy. Cognitive Grammar facilitates testing of important hypotheses in historical linguistics, such as the idea that language change follows an S-shaped curve. The four commitments of Cognitive Grammar furthermore give rise to new hypotheses, such as the idea that analogical change requires semantically homogeneous domains and the cascade hypothesis that language change may form chains whereby a new change starts when a previous change is about to complete. These hypotheses may inform future research in historical linguistics.

The seven case studies indicate that Cognitive Grammar sheds light on a number of important issues in the history of Russian, spanning from Common Slavic and Old Church Slavonic to ongoing change in present-day Russian, and involving change in the sound system as well as in morphosyntax. The case studies address classic problems in Russian and Slavic linguistics such as the jer shift, but also uncover less well-known examples of language change such as the increasing use of the accusative in the decade construction. However, in addition to demonstrating the relevance of Cognitive Grammar for the history of the Russian language, the seven case studies also illustrate the value of Russian as a testing ground for hypotheses in Cognitive Grammar. Cognitive approaches to historical linguistics have been dominated by studies of English. It is high time to go beyond English – other languages have a lot to offer.

# References

Albright, Adam. 2008. Explaining universal tendencies and language particulars in analogical change. In Jeff Good (ed.), *Linguistic Universals and Language Change*. Oxford: Oxford University Press, 144–82.

Albright, Adam. 2009. Modeling analogy as probabilistic grammar. In James P. Blevins and Juliette Blevins (eds.), *Analogy in Grammar: Form and Acquisition*. Oxford: Oxford University Press, 185–213.

Andersen, Henning. 1980. Russian conjugation: Acquisition and evolutive change. In Elizabeth C. Traugott (ed.), *Papers from the 4th International Conference on Historical Linguistics*. Amsterdam: John Benjamins, 285–301.

Andersen, Henning. 2006. Some thoughts on the history of Russian numeral syntax. In Harvey Goldblatt and Nancy Shields Kollmann (eds.), *Rus' Writ Large: Languages, Histories, Cultures. Essays Presented in Honor of Michael S. Flier on His Sixty-Fifth Birthday. Harvard Ukrainian Studies*, 28.1–4, 57–67.

Anderson, Stephen R. 1992. *A-Morphous Morphology*. Cambridge: Cambridge University Press.

Anttila, Raimo. 1989. *Historical and Comparative Linguistics*. 2nd revised ed. Amsterdam: John Benjamins.

Bates, Elizabeth and Brian MacWhinney. 1987. Competition, variation, and language learning. In: Brian MacWhinney (ed.), *Mechanisms of language acquisition*. Hillsdale, NJ: Lawrence Erlbaum Associates, 157–94.

Berdičevskis, Aleksandrs and Hanne Eckhoff. 2014. Verbal constructional profiles: Possibilities and limitations. In Verena Henrich, Erhard Hinrichs, Daniël de Kok, Petya Osenova, and Adam Przepiórkowski (eds.), *Proceedings of the Thirteenth International Workshop on Treebanks and Linguistic Theories (TLT 13)*. Tübingen: University of Tübingen, 2–13.

Bjorvand, Harald. 2000. Diakron lingvistikk. In Rolf Theil Endresen, Hanne Gram Simonsen and Andreas Sveen (eds.), *Innføring i lingvistikk*. Oslo: Universitetsforlaget, 307–39.

Bloomfield, Leonard. 1933. *Language*. New York: Holt, Rinehart and Winston.

Blythe, Richard A. and William Croft. 2012. S-curves and the mechanisms of propagation in language change. *Language* 88.2: 269–304.

Bolinger, Dwight. 1968. Entailment and the meaning of structures. *Glossa: An International Journal of Linguistics* 2: 119–27.

Bybee, Joan L. 1985. *Morphology*. Amsterdam: John Benjamins.

Bybee, Joan L. 2001. *Phonology and Language Use*. Cambridge: Cambridge University Press.

Bybee, Joan L. 2007a. Diachronic linguistics. In Dirk Geeraerts and Hubert Cuyckens (eds.), *The Oxford Handbook of Cognitive Linguistics*. Oxford: Oxford University Press, 945–87.

Bybee, Joan L. 2007b. *Frequency of Use and the Organization of Language*. Oxford: Oxford University Press.

Bybee, Joan L. 2015. *Language Change*. Cambridge: Cambridge University Press.

Bybee, Joan L. 2021. Joint innovation: Integrating speaker and listener in a theory of sound change. Talk given in the series Abralin ao Vivo – Linguists Online, https://aovivo.abralin.org/en/lives/joan-bybee-2/.

Chambers, J. K. 2002. Patterns of variation including change. In J. K. Chambers, Peter Trudgill, and Natalie Schilling-Estes (eds.), *Handbook of Language Variation and Change*. Oxford: Blackwell, 349–72.

Chomsky, Noam. 1986. *Knowledge of Language: Its Nature, Origin, and Use*. New York: Praeger.

Clark, Eve V. 1993. *The Lexicon in Acquisition*. Cambridge: Cambridge University Press.

Comrie, Bernard, Gerald Stone, and Maria Polinsky. 1996. *The Russian Language in the 20th Century*. Oxford: Clarendon Press.

Corbett, Greville G. 1991. *Gender*. Cambridge: Cambridge University Press.

Corbett, Greville G. 1993. The head of Russian numeral expressions. In Greville G. Corbett, Norman M. Fraser, and Scott McGlashan (eds.), *Heads in Grammatical Theory*. Cambridge: Cambridge University Press, 11–35.

Corbett, Greville G. 2006. *Agreement*. Cambridge: Cambridge University Press.

Croft, William. 2000. *Explaining Language Change*. Harlow: Longman.

Cruse, D. Alan. 1986. *Lexical Semantics*. Cambridge: Cambridge University Press.

Dickey, Stephen M. 2000. *Parameters of Slavic Aspect*. Stanford, CA: CSLI.

Diels, Paul. 1963. *Altkirchenslavische Grammatik. Mit einer Auswahl von Texten und einem Wörterbuch. I. Teil: Grammatik*, 2nd ed. Heidelberg: Carl Winter Universitätsverlag.

Diessel, Holger. 2019. *The Grammar Network: How Linguistic Structure is Shaped by Language Use*. Cambridge: Cambridge University Press.

Ding, Nai, Lucia Melloni, Hang Zhang, Xing Tian, and David Poeppel. 2016. Cortical tracking of hierarchical linguistic structures in connected speech. *Nature Neuroscience* 19: 158–64.

Divjak, Dagmar. 2019. *Frequency in Language: Memory, Attention and Learning*. Cambridge: Cambridge University Press.

Fedorenko, Evelina and Cory Shain. 2021 Similarity of computations across domains does not imply shared implementation: The case of language comprehension. *Current Directions in Psychological Science* 30.6: 526–534.

Filin, Fedot P. (ed.). 1972. *Slovar' russkix narodnyx govorov*, vol. 8. Leningrad: Nauka.

Fodor, Jerry A. 1983. *The Modularity of Mind*. Cambridge, MA: The MIT Press.

Gagarina, Natalija. 2003. The early verb development and demarcation of stages in three Russian-speaking children. In Dagmar Bittner, Wolfgang U. Dressler, and Marianne Kilani-Schoch (eds.), *Development of Verb Inflection in First Language Acquisition: A Cross-Linguistic Perspective*. Berlin: Mouton de Gruyter, 131–70.

Geeraerts, Dirk. 2016. The sociosemiotic commitment. *Cognitive Linguistics* 27.4: 527–42.

Geeraerts, Dirk, Gitte Kristiansen, and Yves Peirsman (eds.). 2010. *Advances in Cognitive Socio-Linguistics*. Berlin: De Gruyter Mouton.

Goldberg, Adele E. 1995. *Constructions: A Construction Grammar Approach to Argument Structure*. Chicago: University of Chicago Press.

Goldberg, Adele E. 2006. *Constructions at Work. The Nature of Generalizations in Language*. Oxford: Oxford University Press.

Gor, Kira. 2007. Experimental study of first and second language morphological processing. In Monica Gonzalez-Marquez, Irene Mittelberg, Seana Coulson, and Michael J. Spivey (eds.), *Methods in Cognitive Linguistics*. Amsterdam: John Benjamins, 367–98.

Gor, Kira and Tatiana Chernigovskaya. 2004. Generation of complex verbal morphology in first and second language acquisition: Evidence from Russian. *Nordlyd* 31.6: 819–33.

Gor, Kira and Tatiana Chernigovskaya. 2005. Formal instruction and the acquisition of verbal morphology. In Alex Housen and Michel Pierrard (eds.), *Current Issues in Instructed Second Language Learning*. Berlin: Mouton de Gruyter, 103–36.

Gorbačevič, Kirill S. 1978. *Variativnost' slova i jazykovaja norma*. Leningrad: Nauka.

Gorbachov, Yaroslav V. 2007. Indo-European origins of the nasal inchoative class in Germanic, Baltic and Slavic. Ph.D. dissertation: Harvard University.

Goswami, Usha. 2012. Entraining the brain: Applications to language research and links to musical entrainment. *Empirical Musicology Review* 7.1–2: 57–63.

Graudina, L. K., V. A. Ickovič and L. P. Katlinskaja. 2001. *Grammatičeskij pravil'nost' russkoj reči: stilističeskij slovar' variantov*. Moscow: Nauka.

Haiman, John. 1980. The iconicity of grammar. *Language* 56.3: 515–40.

Hilpert, Martin. 2013. *Constructional Change in English: Developments in Allomorphy, Word Formation, and Syntax*. Cambridge: Cambridge University Press.

Hilpert, Martin. 2015. Historical linguistics. In Ewa Dąbrowska and Dagmar Divjak (eds.), *Handbook of Cognitive Linguistics*. Berlin: De Gruyter Mouton, 346–66.

Hovdenak, Marit, Laurits Killingbergtrø, Arne Lauvhjell et al. 2001. *Nynorskordboka*. Oslo: Det norske samlaget.

Igartua, Ivan and Nerea Madariaga. 2018. The interplay of semantic and formal factors in Russian morphosyntax: Animate paucal constructions in direct object function. *Russian Linguistics* 42.1: 27–55.

Isačenko, Aleksander I. 1974. *Die russische Sprache der Gegenwart: Formenlehre*. Munich: Niemeyer.

Jakobson, Roman. 1936. Beitrag zur allgemeinen Kasuslehre. Gesamtbedeutungen der russischen Kasus. *Travaux du Cercle Linguistique de Prague* 6, 240–88.

Jakobson, Roman. 1948. Russian conjugation, *Word* 4.3: 155–67.

Janda, Laura A. (ed.). 2013. *Cognitive Linguistics: The Quantitative Turn. The Essential Reader*. Berlin: De Gruyter Mouton.

Janda, Laura A. and Steven J. Clancy. 2002. *The Case Book for Russian*. Bloomington, IN: Slavica Publishers.

Janda, Laura A., Anna Endresen, Julia Kuznetsova et al. 2013. *Why Russian Aspectual Prefixes Aren't Empty: Prefixes as Verb Classifiers*. Bloomington, IN: Slavica Publishers.

Janda, Laura A., Olga Lyashevskaya, Tore Nesset, Ekaterina Rakhilina, and Francis M. Tyers. 2018. A constructicon for Russian: Filling in the gaps. In Benjamin Lyngfelt, Lars Borin, Kyoko Ohara, and Tiago Timponi Torrent (eds.), *Constructicography: Constructicon Development across Languages*. [Constructional Approaches to Language 22]. Amsterdam: John Benjamins, 165–81. https://doi.org/10.1075/cal.22.06jan.

Janda, Laura A., Tore Nesset, and R. Harald Baayen. 2010. Capturing correlational structure in Russian paradigms: A case study in logistic mixed-effects modeling, *Corpus Linguistics and Linguistic Theory* 6.1: 29–48.

Joseph, Brian D. 2011. A Localistic Approach to Universals and Variation. In Peter Siemund (ed.), *Linguistic Universals and Language Variation*. Berlin: Mouton de Gruyter, 394–414.

Kager, René. 1999. *Optimality Theory*. Cambridge: Cambridge University Press.

Kemmer, Suzanne. 1993. *The Middle Voice*. Amsterdam: John Benjamins.

Kiparsky, Valentin. 1963. *Russische historische Grammatik* (vol. 1). Heidelberg: Carl Winter Universitätsverlag.

Kiparsky, Valentin. 1967. *Russische historische Grammatik* (vol. 2). Heidelberg: Carl Winter Universitätsverlag.

Kloss, Boris M. 1980. *Nikonovskij svod i russkie letopisi XVI–XVII vekov*. Moscow: Nauka.

Kroch, Anthony. 1989a. Reflexes of grammar in patterns of language change. *Language Variation and Change* 1: 199–244.

Kroch, Anthony. 1989b. Function and grammar in the history of English: Periphrastic *do*. In Ralph W. Fasold and Deborah Schiffrin (eds.), *Language Change and Variation*. Amsterdam: John Benjamins, 133–72.

Kroch, Anthony. 2003. Syntactic change. In Mark Baltin and Chris Collins (eds.), *The Handbook of Contemporary Syntactic Theory*. Oxford: Blackwell, 699–729.

Kuryłowicz, Jerzy. 1995 [1949]. The nature of the so-called analogical processes. Translated into English and with an introduction by Margaret E. Winters. *Diachronica* 12.1: 113–145. [Originally published in 1949 in *Acta Linguistica* 5.17–34].

Kuznetsova, Julia and Anastasia Makarova. 2012. Distribution of two semel-factives in Russian: *-nu* and *-anu*. *Oslo Studies in Language* 4.1: 155–76.

Labov, William. 1994. *Principles of Language Change. Vol. 1: Internal Factors*. Oxford: Blackwell.

Langacker, Ronald W. 1987. *Foundations of Cognitive Grammar*, vol. 1. Stanford, CA: Stanford University Press.

Langacker, Ronald W. 1991a. *Foundations of Cognitive Grammar*, vol. 2. Stanford, CA: Stanford University Press.

Langacker, Ronald W. 1991b. *Concept, Image, and Symbol. The Cognitive Basis of Grammar*. Berlin: Mouton de Gruyter.

Langacker, Ronald W. 1999. *Grammar and Conceptualization*. Berlin: Mouton de Gruyter.

Langacker, Ronald W. 2008. *Cognitive Grammar: A Basic Introduction*. Oxford: Oxford University Press.

Langacker, Ronald W. 2013. *Essentials of Cognitive Grammar*. Oxford: Oxford University Press.

Leopold, Edda. 2005. Diachronie: Grammatik. In Reinhard Köhler, Gabriel Altmann, and Rajmund G. Piotrowski (eds.), *Quantitative Linguistics: An International Handbook*. Berlin: Mouton De Gruyter, 607–33.

Lewandowska-Tomaszczyk, Barbara. 2007. Polysemy, prototypes, and radial categories. In Dirk Geeraerts and Hubert Cuyckens (eds.), *The Oxford Handbook of Cognitive Linguistics*. Oxford: Oxford University Press, 139–69.

London, Justin. 2012. Three things linguists need to know about rhythm and time in music. *Empirical Musicology Review* 7.1–2: 5–11.

Lyashevskaya, Olga N. and Sergey A. Sharoff. 2009. *Častotnyj slovar' sovremennogo russkogo jazyka (na materialax Nacional'nogo korpusa russkogo jazyka)*. Moscow: Azbukovnik.

Lyngfeldt, Benjamin, Lars Borin, Kyoko Ohara, and Tiago Timponi Torrent (eds.). 2018. *Constructicography: Constructicon Development across Languages*. Amsterdam: John Benjamins.

MacNeilage, Peter. 2008. *The Origin of Speech*. Oxford: Oxford University Press.

Mańczak, Witold. 1958. Tendances générales des changements analogiques II. *Lingua* 7: 387–420

Mańczak, Witold. 1980. Laws of analogy. In Jacek Fisiak (ed.), *Historical Morphology*. The Hague: Mouton Publishers, 283–8.

Mathiassen, Terje. 1996. *Russisk grammatikk*. Oslo: Universitetsforlaget.

McCarthy, John J. and Alan Prince. 1993. Generalized alignment. *Yearbook of Morphology* 12: 79–153.

Mel'čuk, Igor A. 1985. *Poverxnostnyj sintaksis russkix čislovyx vyraženij (Wiener Slawistischer Almanach. Sonderband, 16)*. Wien: Institut für Slawistik der Universität Wien.

Nathan, Geoffrey S. 2015. Phonology. In Ewa Dąbrowska and Dagmar Divjak (eds.), *Handbook of Cognitive Linguistics*. Berlin: De Gruyter Mouton, 253–73.

Nesset, Tore. 1996. Affiks eller klitikon? *Norsk lingvistisk tidsskrift* 16: 185–206.

Nesset, Tore. 1998. *Russian Conjugation Revisited*. Oslo: Novus Press.

Nesset, Tore. 2010. Suffix shift in Russian verbs: A case for markedness? *Russian Linguistics* 34.2: 123–38.

Nesset, Tore. 2012. One or several categories? The Old Church Slavonic *no*-verbs and linguistic profiling. *Russian Linguistics* 36: 285–303.

Nesset, Tore. 2013. The history of the Russian semelfactive: The development of a radial category. *Journal of Slavic Linguistics* 21.1: 123–69.

Nesset, Tore. 2015. *How Russian Came to Be the Way It Is: A Student's Guide to the History of the Russian Language*. Bloomington: Slavica Publishers

Nesset, Tore. 2016a. Does historical linguistics need the Cognitive Commitment? Prosodic change in East Slavic. *Cognitive Linguistics* 27.4: 573–85.

Nesset, Tore. 2016b. Russiske rivaler: Cocktailhypotesen. In Hans-Olav Enger, Monica I. Norvik Knoph, Kristian E. Kristoffersen, and Marianne Lind (eds.), *Helt Fabelaktig! Festskrift til Hanne Gram Simonsen på 70-årsdagen*. Oslo: Novus Forlag, 167–80.

Nesset, Tore. 2016c. A FOOTnote to the jers: The Russian trochee-iamb shift and Cognitive Linguistics. *Journal of Slavic Linguistics* 24.2: 359–91. doi: 10.1353/jsl.2016.0015.

Nesset, Tore. 2020. A long birth: The development of gender-specific paucal constructions in Russian. *Diachronica* 37.4: 514–39.

Nesset, Tore and Julia Kuznetsova. 2011. Stability and complexity: Russian suffix shift over time, *Scando-Slavica* 57.2: 268–89.

Nesset, Tore and Julia Kuznetsova. 2015a. Constructions and language change: From genitive to accusative objects in Russian. *Diachronica* 32: 3, 365–96.

Nesset, Tore and Julia Kuznetsova. 2015b. In which case are Russians afraid? *Bojat'sja* with genitive and accusative objects. *Journal of Slavic Linguistics* 23.2: 255–83.

Nesset, Tore and Anastasia Makarova. 2012. 'Nu-drop' in Russian verbs: A corpus-based investigation of morphological variation and change. *Russian Linguistics* 36: 41–63.

Nesset, Tore and Anastasia Makarova. 2014. Testing the semantic homogeneity constraint: Analogical change and Russian verbs. *Journal of Historical Linguistics* 4.2: 161–91.

Nesset, Tore and Anastasia Makarova. 2018. The decade construction rivalry in Russian: Using a corpus to study historical linguistics. *Diachronica* 35.1: 71–106.

Nesset, Tore and Maria Nordrum. 2019. Do Russian paucal numerals govern the genitive? Evidence from stress placement. *Russian Linguistics* 43: 87–105.

Nida, Eugene A. 1958. Analysis of meaning and dictionary making. *International Journal of American Linguistics* 24.4: 279–92.

Nuyts, Jan and Pieter Byloo. 2015. Competing modals: Beyond (inter)subjectification. *Diachronica* 32.1: 34–68.

Padučeva, Elena V. 1996. *Semantičeskie issledovanija*. Moscow: Jazyki russkoj kul'tury.

Pereltsvaig, Asya. 2010. As easy as two, three, four? In Wayles Browne, Adam Cooper, Alison Fisher, Esra Kesici and Nikola Predolac: *Formal Approaches to Slavic Linguistics (FASL-18). The second Cornell meeting 2009* (Michigan Slavic Materials 56). Ann Arbor: University of Michigan, 418–35.

Phillips, Webb and Lera Boroditsky. 2003. Can quirks of grammar affect the way you think? Grammatical gender and object concepts. *Proceedings of the Annual Meeting of the Cognitive Science Society* 25: 928–33.

Rusakova, Marina V. 2013. *Èlementy antropocentričeskoj grammatiki russkogo jazyka*. Moscow: Jazyki slavjanskoj kul'tury.

Saussure, Ferdinand de. 1983 [1916]. *Course in General Linguistics*. Translated and annotated by Roy Harris. London: Duckworth.

Schmid, Hans-Jörg. 2014. Lexico-grammatical patterns, pragmatic associations and discourse frequency. In Thomas Herbst, Hans-Jörg Schmid, and Susen Faulhaber (eds.), *Constructions – Collocations – Patterns*. Berlin: Mouton de Gruyter, 239–93.

Schmid, Hans-Jörg. 2015. A blueprint of the Entrenchment-and-Conventionalization Model. *Yearbook of the German Cognitive Linguistics Association* 3, 1–27.

Schmid, Hans-Jörg. 2016. Why Cogntive Linguistics must embrace the social and pragmatic dimensions of language and how it could do so more seriously. *Cogntive Linguistics* 27.4: 543–58.

Schmid, Hans-Jörg. 2017. A framework for understanding linguistic entrenchment and its psychological foundations. In Hans-Jörg Schmid (ed.), *Entrenchment and the Psychology of Language Learning* . Boston: American Psychological Association Press, 9–35.

Schmid, Hans-Jörg. 2020. *The Dynamics of the Linguistic System: Usage, Conventionalization and Entrenchment*. Oxford: Oxford University Press.

Schuyt, Roel. 1990. *The Morphology of Slavic Verbal Aspect: A Descriptive and Historical Study*. Amsterdam: Rodopi.

*Slovar' russkogo jazyka XI–XVII vv.* 1975–. Moscow: Nauka.

Sommerer, Lotte and Elena Smirnova (eds.). 2020. *Nodes and Networks in Diachronic Construction Grammar*. Amsterdam: John Benjamins.

Sreznevskij, Izmail I. 1893–1906. *Materialy dlja slovarja drevnerusskogo jazyka po pis'mennym pamjatnikam*. St. Petersburg: Tipografija imperatorskoj akademii nauk.

Stang, Christian S. 1942. *Das slavische und baltische Verbum*. Oslo: Det norske vitenskapsakademi.

Steele, Susan. 1978. Word order variation: A typological study. In Joseph Greenberg (ed.), *Universals of Human Language, Vol. 4 Syntax*. Stanford, CA: Stanford University Press, 585–624.

Švedova, Natalija Ju. (ed.). 1980. *Russkaja grammatika*, vol. 2. Moscow: Nauka.

Szymanek, Bogdan. 2005. The latest trends in English word-formation. In Pavol Štekauer and Rochelle Lieber (eds.), *Handbook of Word-Formation*. Dordrecht: Springer, 429–48.

Thelen, Eshter. 1979. Rhythmical stereotypies in normal human infants. *Animal Behaviour* 27: 699–715.

Timberlake, Alan. 1985. Hierarchies in the genitive of negation. In Richard D. Brecht and James S. Levine (eds.), *Case in Slavic*. Columbus, OH: Slavica Publishers, 338–60.

Traugott, Elizabeth Closs and Graeme Trousdale. 2013. *Constructionalization and Constructional Changes*. Oxford: Oxford University Press.

Trehub, Sandra E. and Erin E. Hannon. 2006. Infant music perception: Domain-general or domain-specific mechanisms? *Cognition* 100: 73–99.

Wade, Terence. 1992. *A Comprehensive Grammar of Russian*. Oxford: Blackwell.

Wierzbicka, Anna. 1980. *The Case for Surface Case*. Ann Arbor: Karoma Publishers.

Worth, Dean S. 1984. Russian gen2, loc2 revisited. In Jan Joost van Baak (ed.), *Signs of Friendship*. Amsterdam: Rodopi, 295–306.

Zaliznjak, Andrej A. 2002 [1967]. *Russkoe imennoe slovoizmenenie. S priloženiem izbrannyx rabot po sovremennomu russkomu jazyku i obščemu jazykoznaniju*. Moscow: Jazyki slavjanskoj kul'tury.

Zaliznjak, Andrej A. 2008a. *Drevnerusskie ènklitiki*. Moscow: Jazyki slavjanskix kul'tur.

Zaliznjak, Andrej A. 2008b. '*Slovo o polku Igoreve*': *vzgljad lingvista*. Moscow: Rukopisnye pamjatniki drevnej Rusi.

Zaliznjak, Anna A. and Aleksej D. Šmelev. 2000. *Vvedenie v russkuju aspektologiju*. Moscow: Jazyki russkoj kul'tury.

Žolobov, Oleg F. 2002. Morfosintaksis čislitel'nyx *dva, tri, četyre*: K istorii malogo kvantitativa. *Russian Linguistics* 26.1: 1–27.

# Acknowledgement

I would like to express my gratitude to all the colleagues who have helped me create this Cambridge Element. John Newman, who suggested I write this Element, helped me through the initial phase. Sarah Duffey and Isabel Collins responded quickly to all my queries. Sergey Say and two anonymous reviewers provided invaluable comments on the first version of the manuscript, which led to numerous improvements of the text. I would like to thank all of my co-authors and members of the CLEAR research group at UiT The Arctic University of Norway. Without your contributions I would not have been able to write this Element. Finally, my thanks go to Laura Janda for her endless support on so many levels.

Cambridge Elements ≡

# Cognitive Linguistics

## Sarah Duffy
*Northumbria University*

Sarah Duffy is Senior Lecturer in English Language and Linguistics at Northumbria University. She has published primarily on metaphor interpretation and understanding, and her forthcoming monograph for Cambridge University Press (co-authored with Michele Feist) explores *Time, Metaphor, and Language* from a cognitive science perspective. Sarah is Review Editor of the journal, *Language and Cognition*, and Vice President of the UK Cognitive Linguistics Association.

## Nick Riches
*Newcastle University*

Nick Riches is a Senior Lecturer in Speech and Language Pathology at Newcastle University. His work has investigated language and cognitive processes in children and adolescents with autism and developmental language disorders, and he is particularly interested in usage-based accounts of these populations.

### Editorial Board

### About the Series

Cambridge Elements in Cognitive Linguistics aims to extend the theoretical and methodological boundaries of cognitive linguistics. It will advance and develop established areas of research in the discipline, as well as address areas where it has not traditionally been explored and areas where it has yet to become well-established.

**Cambridge Elements** ≡

# Cognitive Linguistics

### Elements in the Series

*Language Change and Cognitive Linguistics: Case Studies from the History of Russian*
Tore Nesset

A full series listing is available at: www.cambridge.org/ECOG

www.ingramcontent.com/pod-product-compliance
Ingram Content Group UK Ltd.
Pitfield, Milton Keynes, MK11 3LW, UK
UKHW020446010325
455719UK00008B/402